The LOW-FODMAP DIET

THE BEGINNER'S GUIDE
all information you need to have Success on The Low-FODMAP Diet

ROBERT DICKENS & ANITA ROSE

Contents

Introduction 9

   How to Know If You Really Have IBS 10

      Do You Have IBS-C or IBS-D? 12

What Is the Low-FODMAP diet? 14

   The 4 FODMAPS Explained 16

   Benefits of the Low-FODMAP Diet 18

The First Symptoms of Your Gut 20

   Causes of IBS or Alternative Digestive Issues ... 23

      Digestive System 24

      Celiac Disease 25

      Lactose Intolerance 26

      Inflammatory Bowel Disease 28

   Why Women Are More Likely to Get IBS than Men ... 29

How to Overcome IBS 32

   5 Key Steps for Winning the Battle Against IBS ... 35

Keep a food diary 35

Try IBS medications and get rid of unwanted bacteria in your small bowel 37

Tips to Stay on Top of Your Health 42

The Benefits of Vagus Nerve Stimulation for the Digestive System 46

The Importance of the Vagus Nerve 54

6 Practices to Stimulate the Vagus Nerve 56

How to Recognize Vagus Nerve Dysfunction 58

How to Follow the Low-FODMAP Diet 60

Phase 1: Dietary Consultation 62

Phase 2: Reflection and Consideration 66

Phase 3: Planning and Execution 72

Phase 4: High-FODMAPs Elimination 75

FOOD LISTS 77

FRUITS 77

VEGETABLES 78

CEREALS AND FLOURS 80

DAIRY PRODUCT 81

DRIED FRUIT AND SEEDS 82

LEGUMES 83

DRINKS 84

SWEETS AND SWEETENERS	85
CONDIMENTS	85
VEGAN ALTERNATIVES	86

Phase 5: High-FODMAPs Reintroduction 87

Phase 6: Diet and Lifestyle Personalization 88

About the Low-FODMAP Diet 89

Alternative High-FODMAP Options 90

Diet Pitfalls to Avoid 91

FAQ 95

Meal Plan 101

Measurement Conversions 108

BREAKFAST 111

Basic Smoothie Base	112
Basil Omelet with Smashed Tomato VEGETARIAN	114
Crepes and Berries VEGETARIAN	116
Egg Wraps VEGETARIAN	118
Energy Bars VEGETARIAN	120
Fluffy Pancakes VEGETARIAN	122
Green Smoothie VEGAN	124
Kale, Ginger, and Pineapple Smoothie VEGAN	125

Peanut Butter Bowl `VEGETARIAN` ... 126

Quinoa Muffins `VEGETARIAN` ... 128

Quinoa porridge `VEGAN` ... 130

Scrambled Tofu `VEGAN` ... 132

Smoothie Bowl `VEGAN` ... 134

Tomato Omelet `VEGETARIAN` ... 136

LUNCH ... 139

Carrot & Walnut Salad `VEGAN` ... 140

Chicken Wrap ... 142

Parmesan Mayo Corn on the Cob `VEGETARIAN` ... 144

Corn Salad `VEGAN` ... 146

Hawaiian Toasted Sandwich ... 148

Frittata `VEGETARIAN` ... 150

Pesto Toasted Sandwich ... 152

Pineapple, Yogurt on Rice Cakes `VEGETARIAN` ... 154

Quiche in Ham Cups ... 156

Spring Rolls with Satay Sauce `VEGAN` ... 158

Thai Pumpkin Noodle Soup `VEGAN` ... 160

Tomato and Green Bean Salad `VEGETARIAN` ... 162

Tropical Smoothie `VEGAN` ... 164

DINNER ... 167

Baked Chicken Alfredo ... 168

Bolognese ... 170

Burgers 172

Cheesy Chicken 174

Coconut Crusted Fish 176

Beetroot Dip `VEGAN` 178

Vegetable Fried Rice `VEGETARIAN` 180

Day-Before Lamb Stew 182

Pesto Noodles `VEGETARIAN` 184

Pork Tacos with Pineapple Salsa 186

Tofu Skewers `VEGAN` 188

Tuna, Bacon Quinoa Bowl 190

Zucchini Fritters `VEGETARIAN` 192

SNAKS **195**

Chia Pudding `VEGAN` 196

Salted Caramel Pumpkin Seeds `VEGETARIAN` .. 198

Strawberry Ice Cream `VEGAN` 200

Summer Popsicle `VEGAN` 202

Carrot Parsnip Chips `VEGAN` 204

Conclusion **206**

Introduction

Humans have many different needs to support the functionality of the body. These needs are required to sustain various elements that otherwise would deteriorate, stop working, or overall become inefficient, much, such as the digestive system often does.

While irritable bowel syndrome, better known as IBS, is a condition considered to be the worsened case that has evolved from basic digestive issues, it is not something to be taken lightly, especially as we need all the systems in our body to function optimally to survive. The digestive system, for example, is required to turn whole foods into nutrients and energy that the body needs to function properly and repair itself.

Since experiencing digestive issues is a common problem for people, especially in the U.S. due to following a poor diet, it is often not addressed as it comes across as too simple and common for most to deal with. It may not seem like it needs to be treated, but unfortunately, if disrupted or unable to function optimally for an extended period, it can cause IBS, which is a serious condition, and if not treated, could also result in worse conditions. It could affect digestive organs, indicate other potentially harmful conditions present in the body, and in worst-case scenarios, cancer in the digestive tract.

However, any worse-case scenarios can be prevented by treating digestive issues. Whether it seems mild or as though you are displaying symptoms of IBS, it can be managed and treated to ensure your body thrives harmoniously.

If you have digestive issues, it is always necessary to consult with a medical practitioner about your symptoms and concerns. Should you be diagnosed with IBS, there are many options to treat it safely and effectively, which is why I wrote this informative guide to the low-FODMAP diet. This book is aimed to inform you about the IBS condition and how to treat it optimally and benefit from the low-FODMAP diet. I elaborate specifically on the low-FODMAP diet, which is designed to support IBS patients, and explain everything you need to know to manage it effectively while maintaining your health.

Digestive issues may often be brushed underneath the rug and not given the proper diagnosis, attention, and care it needs, but this guide is designed to support your journey in treating IBS.

How to Know If You Really Have IBS

To find out whether you have IBS before starting the low-FODMAP diet, it's best to consult a doctor, but since most people don't, such as visiting the doctor unnecessarily or if you'd, such as to diagnose yourself first and raise the concern with your doctor afterward, consider whether you have IBS or disruptive digestive symptoms.

Since IBS symptoms seem like symptoms everybody experiences at some point due to eating too much or something that doesn't accommodate their body, it can often just be misdiagnosed as just that. However, you can tell whether you actually have IBS and possibly rule out a range of health conditions that a doctor could speculate you to possibly have. Since there is no diagnostic test for

IBS, a doctor will test you for celiac disease, colon cancer, and inflammatory bowel disease when he or she thinks you have IBS. This is only done to ensure that you don't have any other serious conditions, such as those mentioned, which are the most common and severe conditions that could affect your digestive tract alternatively.

Once these tests come back negative, there will only be one potential condition left to diagnose you with, and that is IBS, which can be self-diagnosed if you have recurrent stomach pain, persistent disruptive digestive symptoms, and stool symptoms. Stomach pain can occur at least once or twice weekly and last up to three months, while persistent disruptive digestive symptoms can be diagnosed after six months of experiencing the same symptoms. So, even if your doctor doesn't diagnose you with IBS, if your symptoms remain consistent, you can diagnose yourself. You may also experience stool symptoms, such as issues related to defecation, a change in stool frequency, or any associated changes in stool appearance.

Before considering the low-FODMAP diet, know that it is the second-line dietary measure in people suffering from what they may think is potential IBS. If your body doesn't respond well to a first-line diet strategy, you should switch to the low-FODMAP diet.

What is the first-line diet?

This diet includes a generally healthy approach to eating, only allowing you to include foods into your diet that are considered health-conscious food options. This diet requires you to follow a stable and regular eating pattern and restrict the intake of any possible dietary triggers, including spicy foods, fats, caffeine, and alcohol. A general first-line diet example is the Mediterranean diet, which must be supported by adequate hydration and regular exercise.

Planning for your health while you're changing your diet is equally as important as actually following through with your diet. Since we live in a day and age in which everything is rushed, we often tend to grab food on the go without considering how it's making us feel. In essence, you could be ordering the same meal for lunch every day and feel uncomfortable after eating it but brush it off as normal because you're so used to it. However, in the name of true health, that's not how our bodies should be treated, particularly because we only get one body with a clean bill of health (hopefully) presented to us until we mess it up ourselves.

Whether you're diagnosing yourself or your doctor does it for you, approaching the FODMAP diet should not be a daunting task whatsoever. It can be easier than you think.

Nevertheless, this is only the case if you're prepared. That's why it's important to educate yourself on what you are allowed to eat versus what you're not. It's necessary to find out what groceries you should buy prior to only choosing credible low-FODMAP types of foods. You should also dispose of any high-FODMAP foods in your kitchen, and draw up a shopping list to assist you to the grocery store on your weekly or bi-weekly journey. It's also quite necessary to read menus when dining out in advance and familiarize yourself with options you're allowed to eat to prevent yourself from feeling left out or overwhelmed.

Do You Have IBS-C or IBS-D?

Considering whether your symptoms match the criteria of an IBS patient, there are two types of IBS you could potentially be diagnosed with, IBS-C, which is IBS with constipation that is characterized by abdominal pain; or IBS-D, which is IBS with diarrhea that is characterized by the recurrent or consistent occurrence of diarrhea.

You may also experience symptoms from both types simultaneously. When a doctor diagnoses you, he/she will draw up a conclusion about your diagnostics based on your type of pain or symptoms, which you can then address with treatment measures accordingly. A specific diagnosis is important to ensure you treat it properly and prevent worsening your current condition.

All patients should know that even though IBS is considered a daily lifestyle-altering condition and is permanent, if treated right, you can heal your body of symptoms within three to six months.

IBS-C or IBS-D can be diagnosed with a blood test, which has recently been developed to specify the type of IBS condition in the body. Although treatment options cannot cure the condition, it can treat it and even make you feel, such as you don't have it at all after a few months. However, you do have to keep up with dietary modifications, prescription medications, as well as permanent lifestyle changes to support the management of the condition.

Even though there is no specified diet for all IBS patients, most thrive off the low-FODMAP diet, which includes plenty of fiber, water, and nutrient-rich foods that won't affect your condition negatively. It also excludes carbonated drinks, high-sugar foods, and recommends you to eat more frequent but smaller meals throughout the day.

Once you are diagnosed with a specified type of IBS, it is helpful to consult a gastroenterologist or your primary care physician for the best advice on managing IBS symptoms for the time being, until your body adjusts itself according to your new and improved diet.

What Is the Low-FODMAP diet?

FODMAP refers to a chain of fermentable carbohydrates in the body. It is one of the main causes of general digestive issues, including stomach pain, water retention or bloating, diarrhea, gas, and constipation. All of these symptoms are quite common in the average individual and are experienced more often than people would, such as to admit. It can cause the body to become uncomfortable, which often leaves patients desperate for changing their diets, habits, and overall lifestyle.

Thinking about these symptoms, you may recognize that you've experienced them before, and even though they occur in most people, these are the most general symptoms present in people who have been diagnosed with IBS. That's why, even though it may seem normal or simple, it is necessary to address persistent symptoms related to digestive issues. Now, just because you have these symptoms doesn't mean that you are suffering from IBS, but there is a possibility of getting it if your symptoms continue. This can be cleared up with your doctor.

Although many people don't, such as to visit their doctor, take their advice, or change their lifestyle, IBS should be taken seriously and can be treated effectively in a simple manner.

FODMAP means **Fermentable Oligosaccharides, Disaccharides, Monosaccharides, and Polyols**, all of which are chemical names for a collection of sugars poorly absorbed inside the small intestine. The FODMAP diet is used to treat IBS because the FODMAP chemicals are the main cause of the condition. The collection of sugars causes symptoms such as diarrhea, passing gas, nausea, abdominal pain, constipation, and bloating. It can affect a person's day and even cause them to be less active as it contributes to being uncomfortable, stressed out, and sometimes even embarrassed.

The FODMAP diet is specifically designed to cater to IBS patients because it is very low in fermentable carbs that contain FODMAP sugars. It has been clinically recommended by medical practitioners to treat and manage IBS. Being diagnosed with the condition, you've probably been consuming foods that are high in fermentable carbs, which causes the entire functioning of your digestive tract to become disrupted. If this is the case, adjusting your diet is the best possible treatment for your condition, as well as to restore your health.

The 4 FODMAPS Explained

Fermentable

Oligosaccharides

Carbohydrates in the first FODMAP includes **fructans**, which is a combination of oligosaccharides and inulin, and galactooligosaccharides, which can be found in some of the most popular carbohydrates, such as **rye, wheat, fruits, legumes, and vegetables**. Just because FODMAPs should be consumed in a low quantity does not mean that they are necessarily unhealthy types of food; it's just food your body may not accommodate too well.

Disaccharides

Dairy, or lactose-ingredient products, are considered the main disaccharide that forms a part of FODMAP. It includes foods such as **yogurt, milk, and certain types of cheeses, particularly soft cheese.** You may have heard about people being diagnosed with lactose intolerance, which is the body's direct response to sensitivity to the FODMAP disaccharide.

Monosaccharides

Even though natural sugar is recommended above processed sugar and always will be, some people can be extremely sensitive to fructose, which can be found in different types of **fruit, agave nectar, and the most healing ingredient of all, honey.**

And...

Polyols

The final FODMAP includes carbohydrates, such as **sorbitol, xylitol, and mannitol,** all of which can be found in sugar-free gum and sweeteners. It can also be found in some fruits and vegetables in small quantities.

FODMAPs are present in what we consider as everyday types of food. IBS patients have to recognize what they can eat and what they shouldn't to accommodate their long-term condition. Even though eating a cup of Greek yogurt doesn't seem like it could be harmful to the body, somebody diagnosed with IBS that is very sensitive to disaccharides may have a very painful reaction after eating it, which is why it is very important to recognize what you can eat and what you can't eat. The FODMAP diet focuses on consuming a low quantity to none of these foods, which can support your wellness and help you manage the condition much more easily.

Benefits of the Low-FODMAP Diet

1 Reduced digestive discomfort and disruptions

The low-FODMAP diet can treat IBS symptoms, which include mild to severe stomach pain, bloating, acid reflux, bowel urgency, lack of bowel movements, and flatulence. Since stomach pain is one of the main symptoms and affects over 80% of people diagnosed with IBS, making diet adjustments by cutting out low-FODMAP foods can relieve pain and stomach bloating. According to a study, IBS patients reported having so much pain that they would trade 25% of their lives just to be completely symptom-free. IBS symptoms can become extremely severe and can be treated successfully with the low-FODMAP diet (Healthline, 2017).

2 Improved quality of life

Whether IBS symptoms are mild or severe, it can be very debilitating and prevent people from actually living their lives to the fullest. Since the low-FODMAP diet improves the condition's symptoms, it can change one's life by also increasing energy levels and boosting your mood. It can improve your psychological relationship with your condition and help you appreciate what it means to live a healthy lifestyle that is catered to fulfilling your body's daily needs, which is very important.

3 Weight Loss and increased confidence

The low-FODMAP diet is not a "diet for weight-loss." However, it does contribute to weight loss if you are storing excess weight due to your current diet, habits, and lack of engaging in physical activity. Since IBS causes a lack of energy and a general feeling of being uncomfortable, you may not feel motivated to move your body. In fact, anyone diagnosed with IBS knows how difficult it is to maintain their confidence altogether, especially when they are bloated daily or struggling to lose weight. With up to 54% of people living with IBS that are left with a sense of self-consciousness about their looks, losing weight, even if it's just water weight that causes bloating, will help you feel better about your image, which will improve self-esteem and your overall confidence to thrive in the world (Rachel Pauls Food, 2017).

The First Symptoms of Your Gut

It has been established that foods high in FODMAPs can have adverse effects on the body and can cause gut symptoms by drawing fluid deep into the intestines or through bacterial fermentation. When fluid is drawn into the intestine, water is pulled from the body tissue and fills up the intestines, which essentially causes bloating or more intense gut symptoms, such as diarrhea in anyone whose body responds in a sensitive manner to certain types of food.

Since FODMAPs consist of short-chain sugars, they become osmotically active in the body. When eating fructose, for instance, a sensitive response to it could cause twice as much water to enter the intestine than glucose, which is not listed as a FODMAP. Given that fructose forms part of FODMAPs, you can see that one cannot list sugar as a type of food that causes negative or reactive gut symptoms in the body. Instead, FODMAPs are narrowed down to specific types of food, such as fructose. Those who are diagnosed with IBS will have to adjust their diets entirely due to the effects FODMAPs have on the body, and with their condition, their symptoms ultimately increase and worsen because of their sensitivity to food.

With bacterial fermentation, the gut is affected mainly by carbohydrates, which need to be processed and broken down into simple individual sugars in the body. This is done primarily by enzymes and occurs before it can be absorbed by your body's intestinal wall to create energy in the body. Since we can't produce all of the enzymes required to break FODMAPs down in the body, it may result in undigested FODMAPs that make its way to the colon, small intestine, or large intestine, which causes the digestive tract to become disrupted.

Since the food we eat first enters our large intestine before reaching the small intestine, the presence of bacteria that ferments foods in the large intestine is responsible for the processing of food in the digestive tract, making it possible for the body to properly digest everything we consume. When the body doesn't accommodate certain foods, the presence of the bacteria can cause the body to release chemicals and gas that may lead to serious digestive symptoms, including stomach pain, bloating and irregular bowel movements. Needless to say, adjusting your diet will cause your body to gradually become healthier from the inside out; call it a reintroduction to a harmonious environment if you must. To reach a point in which your body isn't negatively affected by the food you eat is a really good and balanced point to reach with your diet.

Inulin is another FODMAP that can also upset the large intestine and is responsible for producing up to 70% more gas than the over-consumption of glucose in the body.

Now, similar symptoms in IBS patients are also experienced in non-IBS patients, and the reason is that most people are merely sensitive to some types of food. In this case, doctors usually diagnose people that don't have IBS but are relatively symptomatic with colonic hypersensitivity.

The FODMAP diet can assist IBS-diagnosed and colonic hypersensitive individuals by reducing gut symptoms caused by eating the wrong types of food for the body. Following a low-FODMAP diet doesn't mean you'll have to quit your favorite foods altogether, but it does mean you have to consume the specified low-FODMAP foods instead of high FODMAPS, which is generally consumed daily by the average individual. By following this diet, you will not only be able to relieve gut symptoms, such as digestive symptoms, cramping, bloating, food intolerance, abdominal pain, gas, and altered bowel habits, but you'll also be able to improve the quality of your life, which is something every single individual should be striving toward achieving. Since we only have one body, it is incredibly necessary to nurture it and look after it, especially if we have neglected to do so for a long time. Whether you're overweight, suffering from obesity, underweight, or even healthy, suffering from IBS symptoms will disrupt your life and your goals to look and feel great.

Once you start the low-FODMAP diet, you should know that above all else, you really don't have to completely eliminate foods from your diet. Often, society tends to consume more than they should of what's bad for them, such as coffee, sugar, or particularly, dairy, which is something most people have a hypersensitive response to. It's important to recognize what your body responds to and how it affects your day because if you continue to consume food that is not for your body, it could end up causing you more harm than good. Although it is not easy to follow any given diet, since the low-FODMAP diet doesn't require you to eliminate foods but just reduce the intake thereof instead, it is perfect for any individual that suffers from IBS or related digestive disorders. There is an elimination phase included in this diet, which is only focused on eliminating more than the daily recommended amount of high-FODMAP foods, as well as those you could potentially be intolerant to.

If you're embarking on a new diet to improve your health, you should be aware that this diet isn't considered a gluten-free diet; however, it is quite low in gluten due to the disruptive effects gluten has on most individuals that experience predominant symptoms of bloating and gas. Since the diet restricts wheat-based products, it is mostly gluten-free as gluten is mainly found in wheat. Wheat is excluded from the low-FODMAP diet because of its high content of fructans, which is a disruptive contributing element to IBS.

When it comes to everyone's favorite and most-difficult-to-kick types of foods, dairy sure does take the cake, especially when it comes to milk, cheese, ice-cream, chocolate, butter, and the list goes on... Luckily, this diet does not eliminate dairy either; it does, however, restrict high quantities of lactose that are typically present in most dairy products and could disrupt the digestion of lactose-intolerant individuals. Nevertheless, there are dairy products that have low lactose levels, which makes them low-FODMAP and possible for you to include in your diet. Low-FODMAP dairy foods include sour cream, hard or aged cheeses, and a popular for most, creme fraiche.

Starting out this diet, there is a lot of relief found in the fact that low-FODMAP diets are also not considered long-term diets. The diet is not recommended to be followed for more than eight weeks. It's just a diet designed to treat and improve gut symptoms, ultimately reintroducing a better way of eating for IBS-diagnosed individuals, as well as anyone struggling with digestive disorders. Once you've tried out the low-FODMAP diet for anywhere between six to eight weeks, you will discover that your gut symptoms have improved, which will allow you to also make better decisions when it comes to food options. Even though you are not recommended to follow the diet for longer than eight weeks at a time, it will surely set your mind and body in the habit of eating foods that accommodate your body, and also help you recognize which foods should be consumed in a lower quantity.

Causes of IBS or Alternative Digestive Issues

IBS may present mild symptoms, such as stomach pain, gas, bloating, and possibly indigestion, in the beginning stages of the condition, but it goes untreated, it could escalate into something more severe. Since humans are highly interested in discovering the origin of illnesses and infections to prevent possibly being diagnosed with conditions it's relatively frustrating to think that there is no single established cause for the condition that can be treated with prescription medication.

Given that this is the case, each person experiences the effects of IBS differently, and even recover from it in various ways by implementing different techniques. No matter the cause of your condition, however, it is serious, and unless treated, it can worsen, which can lead to one living a very uncomfortable life. Most doctors believe that the primary cause in most patients includes factors such as the gastrointestinal tract mobility, increased pain sensitivity, food intolerances, and irregular nervous system signals in the body. Even though doctors try, they often struggle to pinpoint the cause of the condition in IBS-C and IBS-D in patients.

The digestive system can endure the effects of IBS, celiac disease, lactose intolerance, and inflammatory bowel disease, all of which can contribute as causes to a disruptive digestive system. That means that just because you have digestive symptoms doesn't mean you have IBS, although IBS will always be considered as a potential underlying condition everyone can be diagnosed with.

Potential causes of poor gut health and digestive conditions explained:

Digestive System

- Abnormal small intestine and colon movements, which can either be unbalanced, too fast or too slow

- Gastroenteritis, otherwise known as stomach flu, a bacterial infection of the intestines and stomach, which could trigger IBS symptoms or hypersensitivity in the colon

- Food sensitivities, mainly caused by the lack of absorption of acids and sugars in foods

- Hypersensitivity from gas or bowel movements

- Anxiety, depression, somatic symptom disorder, which has been found to be a direct diagnosis of IBS, mainly due to recurrent stress in the body

- Stressful early life events, including physical or sexual abuse

- SIBO (small intestinal bacterial overgrowth)

- Reproductive hormones or unbalanced neurotransmitters in the brain

- **Gluten and Lactose intolerance**

Celiac Disease

This condition is presented with three main symptoms that are quite serious. It includes constipation, diarrhea, and abdominal pain, and even though it forms a part of IBS-listed symptoms, it can also indicate celiac disease alone. Since it is often difficult to diagnose, these conditions are often confused with one another. According to studies by Allesio Fasano, director of the University of Maryland Center for Celiac Research, 5% to 15% of diagnosed cases have originally been misdiagnosed as IBS.

However, IBS is a syndrome and includes specified symptoms, whereas celiac disease is a disease with three main symptoms, along with countless underlying and potentially dangerous symptoms. While IBS symptoms can be experienced every day, celiac disease can damage your intestines without you feeling it, such as when you don't have any symptoms at all. In IBS, symptoms are always set, while celiac disease can have you display anything from osteoporosis, dental defects, and joint pain, all of which you won't experience with IBS.

Celiac disease is thus known for its notorious lack of symptoms. This may seem like a good thing as it doesn't have the same painful effect on the body as IBS, right?

However, in retrospect, if you don't recognize that you may potentially have celiac disease, you could only seek medical advice from your doctor once the disease intensifies, which could be very damaging to your digestive tract, particularly your intestines. One of celiac disease's main underlying symptoms is gastrointestinal symptoms. If you don't have physical symptoms indicating internal intestinal issues, then you can scratch IBS off your list of conditions you're likely to have.

With IBS, you will realize you have it due to the consistent display of symptoms in the body. It's also important to note that, with IBS, your intestines will work by implementing a squeezing pattern that will cause discomfort, which is how you'll know whether you have the syndrome. With celiac disease, the manner in which the bowels move are not affected. Celiac disease is best described as a peculiar autoimmune disorder that damages the intestines from the inside. It is asymptomatic as far as those who have it are concerned.

When you experience any discomfort related to your digestive system, it can be symptomatic (IBS) or asymptomatic (celiac disease). If you test for both these conditions and don't have either, then you could potentially have gluten sensitivity, which is a reaction to gluten. In this case, you can have one of two reactions, including a gluten allergy and gluten sensitivity. Gluten allergies are not likely to cause any symptoms related to gluten intolerance, while gluten sensitivity will display similar symptoms to IBS. This can be self-diagnosable if you display any IBS-related symptoms after eating foods that contain wheat, which can be diagnosed as gluten sensitivity. Testing for gluten sensitivity, it is important to consider that celiac disease displays a similar response in the body to gluten.

Distinguishing whether you have IBS, celiac disease, or gluten sensitivity/allergies, can be a time-consuming experience. The right diagnoses for these diseases, particularly celiac disease, is quite important, and you should ensure you get the correct diagnosis from your doctor or perhaps even more than one doctor.

How the low-FODMAP diet helps your diagnosis: You can adjust your diet and remove high-FODMAP from it to see what your body responds to best before seeking advice from a gastroenterologist, who can properly diagnose you after you've measured the effects the low-FODMAP diet has on your body.

Lactose Intolerance

Although recognized as having a somewhat similar effect on the body, presenting the same type of symptoms, particularly in the digestive tract and gut, there are still some differences between the two conditions, as well as simple treatment options on how to manage it.

Lactose intolerance can be self-diagnosed by simply quitting dairy for a few days and checking whether any symptoms, including bloating, gas, stomach pain, or diarrhea, are relieved compared to days when you consume low to high quantities of dairy. After consuming dairy products, symptoms can occur within 30 minutes to 2 hours. The best indication of whether you have lactose intolerance is feeling better and managing to relieve your symptoms after quitting dairy for a few days. The condition can be self-diagnosed and treated accordingly by avoiding dairy altogether. You can also consult your doctor to test your body's sensitivity to lactose with a simple physical exam, reviewing your family history, or having you complete a hydrogen breath test, which will test the presence of gas caused by dairy in your body. Your doctor will consult you about your family history, as lactose intolerance can be linked to other degenerative diseases passed on to you, such as celiac disease, ulcerative colitis, and Crohn's disease. Should you test positive for lactose intolerance, your doctor will recommend you get tested for related potential conditions as well.

Since symptoms of IBS and lactose intolerance are quite similar, both of which include constipation and the body's inability to empty the colon properly, it's necessary to get diagnosed for IBS or lactose intolerance so that you can treat the condition accordingly. Both conditions can become very painful and cause your days to be very uncomfortable.

Perhaps the biggest difference between IBS and lactose intolerance is that the causes of lactose intolerance are known, along with treatment options for it as opposed to IBS, which can be caused by a number of factors. More doctors, however, believe that a spastic or compromised colon that cannot move waste properly through the digestive tract is considered the main source of IBS. This is believed to occur due to a disconnect between signals in the brain that struggle to connect with nerves in the gut. Apart from the differentiation of causes between the two conditions, doctors also believe that genes, intestinal infections, and long-term stress can contribute to a worsening state of IBS, whereas these contributing factors don't affect, nor aggravate lactose intolerance(WebMD, n.d.)

Inflammatory Bowel Disease

This condition, otherwise known as IBD, is quite similar to IBS due to commonly shared symptoms, including cramping, abdominal pain, and frequent or urgent bowel movements. Despite the two conditions sharing similar symptoms, they are quite different, as IBS is a disorder that can be found affecting the gastrointestinal (GI) tract, while IBD affects the bowel wall, usually inflaming or damaging it. This can lead to growth sores and intestinal narrowing which can become quite painful. When patients are diagnosed with both bowel conditions IBS and IBD, it also becomes relatively dangerous and should be addressed immediately.

IBS can be tested with a simple blood test, while IBD, including diseases such as ulcerative colitis and Crohn's disease, can be complex and take several months to diagnose. Once a patient's family and medical history have been reviewed, it is followed with a physical exam, a few laboratory tests, and then a range of endoscopic procedures. Several blood tests can help doctors distinguish between various forms, along with the severity of IBD, paired with the best possible treatment for the condition. In some cases, an MRI or CT scan can also be used for confirming the correct diagnosis. It may even give doctors enough information to see how much of a patient's intestine is affected.

Just like IBS, IBD must be treated carefully; this includes the management of symptoms with the use of prescription antibiotics, antidiarrheal drugs, dietary and lifestyle changes, such as integrating more low-FODMAP foods into one's diet, and as a more extreme option, surgery.

Both of these conditions can be treated individually and collectively. However, it's always best to treat it as soon as possible, before you develop both conditions simultaneously.

Why Women Are More Likely to Get IBS than Men

IBS has reportedly a female-male ratio of 2-2.5:1, a statistic based only on those who seek medical advice. This study is relevant to the U.S. alone and can be different depending on geography, race, community bases, as well as whether studies are performed in primary or tertiary medical settings globally. Apart from IBS, there is a range of gastrointestinal disorders that affect both men and women every day, but particularly women. This is especially true as women's bodies tend to handle the condition much differently than men. Studies have found that women were found to be less susceptible to visit their doctor than men, which is due to gender-related features found in the brain. The study conducted by researcher Tanja Babic at the Penn State Hershey College of Medicine suggested that nerve cells have the ability to control the means in which food travels through the intestines, which for women tend to be slower and at times, more disruptive than it is for men and is also due to the functioning of the brain (Science Daily, 2015).

She explained that the chances of women developing IBS or gastrointestinal disorders are greater than they are for men and that there are reasons to support this statement. She continued saying that women have a different brain structure and functioning than men, which includes much higher GABA levels (y-aminobutyric acid), a type of inhibitory neurotransmitter. **GABA** has an effect on neuron activity and is responsible for maintaining control of digestion.

The investigation was conducted to test whether GABA activity found in these neurotransmitters are different in women and men. The study was conducted to pinpoint whether it can be changed, and if it can, to prove that it would allow for the availability of improved treatment for women diagnosed with gastrointestinal disorders. Testing rats to identify differences between the two, the nerve signal received from nerves and the brain, along with its responsiveness to signals found that nerves found in female rats received a lot more signals responsible for suppressing the intestinal movement of food than in male rats. Nerves were also found to be less responsive once stimulated. Data provided proves that nerves in control of the intestines in women are slower and receive a lot more inhibitory signals transported from the brain, which explains why digestion in women is often more compromised than in men.

Reviewing this study, it's easy to see why a potential clinical presentation of gastrointestinal and IBS symptoms, along with treatment strategies, can differ in both women and men. Research also suggests that the IBS sub-type, constipation, occurs in more women than men. With any digestive-related disorder, gender and sex hormones play a prevalent role, all of which contribute to the pathophysiology that makes up IBS (Science Daily, 2015).

When it comes to the symptoms experienced by women as opposed to men, **women experience more depression, anxiety, fatigue**, and feel as though their quality of life is reduced with IBS than men. Due to the extent of the condition having more relevance and a greater impact on women than in men, fewer men participate in clinical trials for drug testing for IBS than women. By establishing the differences in the effects of IBS on the body in women and men, medical practitioners can become more accurate with their diagnosis for both genders and potentially improve treatment options for IBS.

Looking at hormonal factors, women and men are obviously also affected differently in various other aspects, especially when gut motility, stress responses, as well as visceral pain perception when interacting with neuromodulators and emotional systems are considered. In women, estrogen and progesterone can inhibit smooth muscle contractions, which can cause more stomach pain, among other symptoms, than in men. It is also a fact that women experience more constipation regularly than men, apart from during their menstrual periods when their ovarian hormones are relatively low. Women are also found to have slower gastrointestinal transit and a delayed colonic transit when their ovarian hormone levels are increased.

Although women are more prone to experience issues with digestion, such as constipation, IBS or gastrointestinal disorders, the low-FODMAP diet is designed to treat IBS and related digestive disorders in both genders. However, it is specifically helpful for women, taking into consideration the range of factors they face in the battle against IBS.

How to Overcome IBS

Remember:

Stomach is the engine of our body and the bowel is us second brain

Irritable Bowel Syndrome is a condition that presents a very uncomfortable and debilitating condition that is often accompanied by pain in the abdomen, along with the loss of energy, mental fatigue, and just an overall feeling of hopelessness. If you think that curing IBS is as easy as visiting your local pharmacy and taking some antacids or some type of laxative to relieve constipation, you're wrong. Treating IBS starts with changing your diet, but also visiting your doctor, who can formally diagnose you.

As mentioned, IBS can be misdiagnosed as a few other conditions due to extreme similarities between conditions, especially celiac disease, lactose intolerance, irritable bowel disease (IBD), and other gastrointestinal disorders. IBS is not a simple condition, and it should not be treated as such.

As an IBS patient, you may feel the need to use a bathroom frequently. If you are not diagnosed with IBS yet, using the bathroom more than a few to several times a day as per usual can indicate that you potentially have IBS. The reason why people feel uncomfortable with the condition is that going out or even simply going to work seems risky as they need to use the bathroom far too often. This may affect one's life in a bigger way than most people think, and due to the extent of the diagnosis, it even keeps some individuals from living their lives and participating in daily activities.

Looking for self-help remedies, IBS patients tend to turn to adjusting their diet and lifestyle first. Most individuals refrain from integrating exercise into their daily life because of adverse symptoms, such as stomach pain and diarrhea. People with IBS often don't know what they should and shouldn't eat but start cutting out foods from their diet they think contributes to their condition, including dairy and gluten. Cutting out several types of everyday foods, or foods most people enjoy, such as pasta, pizza, sugar, and bread, IBS patients are likely to develop anxiety, experience discomfort, visceral hypersensitivity, and overall social distancing. The irony of developing these symptoms and fears is that it also contributes to worsening gastrointestinal sensations, which creates a ripple effect, ultimately causing patients to lose hope in the maintenance and recovery of IBS. Some people with IBS may also feel excruciating pain and humiliation, which again, can restrict their quality of life.

Treating IBS is essential for living your best life. There are a few treatment options to choose from, all of which have been tried by IBS patients before and have also been tested in clinical trials that involved dozens of people with different variations of IBS. By implementing these treatment options, symptoms can be relieved and wellness restored. One of the most effective options includes the low-FODMAP diet, which works best when combined with cognitive-behavioral therapy (CBT), an alternative treatment option that has been found to deliver very effective results. When deciding to implement this option as a form of treatment, however, people with IBS must ensure they don't mistake IBS with another condition, such as inflammatory bowel disease, lactose intolerance, or IBD. This is very important, which is why your doctor must formally declare that you have IBS before you proceed with options to treat it. Inflammatory bowel disease especially, including colitis, Crohn's disease, and celiac disease, is a very serious condition, which can be ruled out by conducting stool and blood tests by your doctor.

Once you have established that you have IBS and not other diseases, you must understand IBS and the powerful link between the arousal of the sympathetic nervous system and stress, which acts as one of the key triggers for gastrointestinal discomfort, including pain and intestinal tract dysfunction. Stress can also worsen intestinal conditions, and to manage it to relieve symptoms successfully, IBS patients must learn relaxation techniques to combat it. Practicing deep breathing or going for a daily 20-minute walk are just two examples of managing stress successfully.

To use different methods to manage IBS, including CBT and dietary changes, one must be able to get their body at a point of relaxation that supports the recovery of the intestinal tract and digestive system. To relax the body, the mind must re-access its beliefs, which cannot include fear or inaccurate or negative beliefs about gastrointestinal symptoms and disorders. For instance, your body cannot benefit, nor recover from IBS if it is stressed out or actively responding to a lot of stressors, especially because this can cause a hostile environment inside the body, particularly causing a spastic colon that worsens IBS and can create a space for even worse conditions to emerge. To avoid this, behavioral experiments can also be conducted to adjust your way of thinking about your condition or health. This can be done with meditation, exercise, and by integrating positive affirmations into your life.

Apart from protecting your internal organs and digestive tract, it can also reduce anxiety and depression, which can literally push someone to go out and participate in society or become social again. By identifying what is accurate in the mind and what is made up of our own thoughts and self-loathing, IBS patients can discover that going out and visiting the bathroom elsewhere, as simple as though it may sound, is indeed not a big deal whatsoever. This could significantly change a patient's quality of life.

With CBT exposure therapy, apart from reaching a point of relaxing the mind and internal body, a patient will start to do the things they've been avoiding, which may start out small but could turn into something as big as spending half a day out and about, enjoying life and performing daily activities.

5 Key Steps for Winning the Battle Against IBS

Keep a food diary

Since this low-FODMAP guide is all about adjusting your diet to fit your body's needs to combat IBS, just as it is important to alter your eating habits, it's necessary to record everything you eat too. Now, if you're not big on journaling, it's totally relatable. The point of recording your meals is not to good-cop or bad-cop yourself after each day or week, checking how many things you ate right or wrong, but the point is to see how what you ate affected you on different days, as well as various times of the day.

To further test the extensity of IBS in the beginning stages of your diagnosis, it is recommended to document your snacks and meals every day, along with the time of day and how it made you feel after you ate it, which can be completed right before consuming your next snack or meal. If you eat dairy in a certain quantity for breakfast that is comfortable for your body, but you follow it up the next day with double the quantity of dairy and feel sick, you should know that one small serving of dairy per day is probably welcomed by your body. Since the point of the low-FODMAP diet is not to eliminate foods altogether from your diet, you can become resourceful and still enjoy your favorite foods in small quantities once or twice a week. The goal of the low-FODMAP diet isn't to be strict or reach a goal, but it is to improve your quality of life, maintain a healthy diet, and allow your diet to work for you in the best way possible while treating potential symptoms that occur in your body due to eating certain types of food.

Recording your meals, you will also be able to identify which foods improve your symptoms, which can be a good indication of what you should be focusing on and including in your diet. By tracking your symptoms every week, you can gradually see whether your diet alterations are improving your condition.

According to the National Institute of Diabetes and Digestive and Kidney Diseases, avoiding milk-based products, caffeine, high-fat foods, alcohol, artificial sweeteners (also dietary sodas and snacks), beans, cabbage, and any other gas-inflicting vegetables can be helpful. It is also recommended to consume fiber, nuts, and chocolate in low quantities. Should it aggravate IBS symptoms, it should be avoided altogether.

Even though fiber-based foods can potentially worsen symptoms in IBS patients, it is recommended to increase fiber intake to see if it improves symptoms as opposed to worsening your condition. It can reduce constipation that has resulted from IBS, with the best fiber-rich foods including fruit, vegetables, some legumes, and whole grains. IBS patients are recommended to consume between 22 and 34 grams of fiber daily; however, it must be added to your diet slowly, only 2 to 3 grams every day, gradually building up to a higher daily intake of fiber that must eventually remain consistent to avoid any potential digestive disruptions. Adding high quantities of fiber to your diet too fast can cause stomach pain, bloating, and gas. The only way to keep track of your fiber intake, along with keeping your diet clean, is by writing down what you've eaten during the day, or even better, pre-planning your meals to ensure you have a schedule of meals to stick to.

Additionally, because the low-FODMAP diet is recommended for all IBS patients, by learning what triggers your gut, you will be able to identify exactly why the low-FODMAP diet is perfectly tailored to suit your daily needs.

Try IBS medications and get rid of unwanted bacteria in your small bowel

Since doctors aren't sure about the direct cause of irritable bowel syndrome, people with IBS are usually prescribed medications that work by relieving symptoms, ultimately allowing them to live the most normal life they possibly can. Should you alter your diet or adopt the low-FODMAP diet but still experience adverse symptoms, or even mild symptoms, you can turn to medication to assist you along the way. Since stress plays a major role as a potential cause of IBS, it is also recommended to reduce your stress levels to see whether your symptoms improve before trying medications.

Trying IBS medications, you can decide how natural or unnatural you'd like your treatment options to be. Medication proven effective to reduce IBS symptoms include:

- **Fiber supplements**
  Methylcellulose (Citrucel) or Psyllium (Metamucil), both of which alleviates constipation

- **Anti-diarrheal medications**
  Loperamide (Imodium), used to reduce symptoms of diarrhea

- **Laxatives** (Osmotic)
  Polyethylene glycol or milk of magnesia, to treat constipation

- **Antispasmodic medications**
  Dicyclomine (Bentyl) or hyoscyamine (Levsin) to reduce bowel spasms

- **Antibiotics**
  Rifaximin (Xifaxan) to treat bacterial overgrowth in the small intestine.

- **Antidepressant medications**

Tricyclic antidepressants or serotonin reuptake inhibitors to relieve depression, anxiety, or physical pain

- **Peppermint oil capsules**

  To treat and alleviate all symptoms of IBS

- **Alosetron**

  Lotronex to relax the colon or to slow down waste movement through the small bowel, which is used to reduce stomach pain and diarrhea

- **Eluxadoline**

  Viberzi to reduce the inconsistency of stools and reduce stomach pain

- **Lubiprostone**

  Amitiza to increase the secretion of fluids within the small intestine, which assists the movement of stool in the intestines

- **Linaclotide**

  Linzess, a powerful pain reliever, that works by blocking pain signals, ultimately increasing the size of passages in the intestines to allow contents in the gastrointestinal tract to move through it more easily

- **Probiotics**

  To support the protective layer of the stomach when using medications to treat the gastrointestinal tract, especially when taking antibiotics.

Apart from the above-mentioned medications, all of which can be prescribed to you by your doctor, you may also benefit from ensuring there are no unnecessary bacteria in the small bowel. To treat the small bowel, you can request rifaximin (Xifaxan), prescribed as two 200 mg tablets that can be taken three times a day on a trial of seven to ten days. This medication is used to combat chronic bacterial overgrowth responsible for IBS symptoms, such as bloating. Additionally, you can also request an antifungal, such as fluconazole or nystatin that can be taken for up to four weeks to ensure your small bowel is free of pathogens or unwanted bacteria.

Alleviate psychological or physical stressors in the body

The human body cannot thrive in a hostile environment. This statement is incredibly true, outwardly and internally.

When stress affects your life, you have probably come to find that you need to deal with it to be able to live your best life; otherwise, you may catch yourself constantly worrying about everything, which can affect your mood, mental health, sleeping patterns, and overall quality of life. Just as stress has an outer effect on the body, it equally has an internal effect that can cause massive disturbance to your internal organs, systems in your body, and an adverse interaction between your brain and digestive tract, which ultimately worsens IBS symptoms. Needless to say, stress can have a very negative effect on the body, and it usually starts by affecting your digestion first.

It is recommended to incorporate relaxation techniques into your daily life to assist symptom relief and improve your wellbeing. Taking off the pressure of long meditation sessions, which is definitely something to work up to, you can start off by spending five to ten minutes a day by solely focusing on nothing, accompanied by deep breathing exercises, taking a timeout from your strenuous thoughts and responsibilities. Abdominal breathing sounds like a very simple thing to integrate into your life, and you may even think, "But, I breathe every minute of every day." However, it's not the same as practicing deep abdominal breathing, visualization, and muscle relaxation, which can benefit you in many helpful ways, including improving your sleep, decreasing overall fatigue, reducing anxiety, reducing muscle tension, improving concentration, memory, productivity, and boosting your energy levels. Practicing mediation, adopting a daily active lifestyle, focusing on getting enough sleep, and even seeking support from a doctor or counselor about how to reduce stress in the body can help you deal with and overcome IBS.

Move your body regularly

Exercising is often linked to only losing weight, but did you know that you need to exercise or become physically active at least a few times a week to ensure your body remains in good working condition?

So, about the stigma of weight-loss and working out, losing weight doesn't necessarily phase IBS patients, particularly because they focus on their health issues and relieving their symptoms, but what if exercise has been the answer to improving your physical health all along?

It's true, exercising can relieve symptoms related to IBS, particularly because it aids in stimulating the normal contractions of the intestines but also reduces stress, both of which decrease IBS symptoms, including bloating and stomach pain caused by a poorly functioning metabolism. Exercising for just 20 minutes a day a few times a week, can also improve your overall quality of life and prevent IBS symptoms from getting worse.

Seek psychological assistance

It sounds silly, but seeking psychological assistance from a therapist can aid in helping one cope with the mental toll IBS takes on the body. Any condition that alters one's life can also have a major impact on mental wellbeing, which can be treated with talking therapy, especially cognitive-behavioral therapy (CBT). This type of therapy is recommended by a healthcare professional in the treatment process of IBS. CBT is focused on the actions and thoughts of one's emotions, which has a direct impact on the symptoms of IBS. Since CBT introduces relaxation techniques and focuses on stress management, it is proven efficient in overcoming IBS.

Similar psychological therapies that are positive options include mindfulness training and gut-related therapy. Hypnotherapy can improve anxiety related to IBS, gastrointestinal symptoms, depression, and a patient's quality of life. Hypnosis can be used to relax the colon muscles, ultimately to regain control of your body and physiological responses.

Mindfulness training can treat IBS by shifting one's focus to sensations in the body, allowing one to learn how to become present and feel in control instead of worrying about sensations that cannot be controlled or focusing on being too aware of IBS symptoms and how it affects one's everyday life. Instead, mindfulness training can help a patient focus on improving his/her health and living their best possible life while improving their symptoms daily.

Tips to Stay on Top of Your Health

If you're living with IBS, it can often feel like you're alive but only going through the motions of life every single day. Even though you're breathing and performing your daily routine, you may feel like you're missing out on life, along with the quality that's supposed to accompany it. If you're experiencing severe symptoms that include stomach pain after each meal, it can leave you hopeless as you try to piece back together elements in your life. IBS is a very self-limiting condition, and because there are many factors to consider living with IBS, it's important to know that there are indeed things you can do that will aid in improving your life. Whether you're recovering from a gastrointestinal disorder or a few digestive issues, recovery is always a possibility.

Eliminate certain types of food

Even though food isn't medically considered the main cause of IBS symptoms, it does play the biggest role as a contributing factor that causes symptoms in the body. The best way to tell whether food is affecting you in a negative way is by checking which foods cause bloating after consuming it. Foods that cause bloating and gas usually include cabbage, Brussel sprouts, and cauliflower. If you're experiencing IBS symptoms after eating these foods, eliminate them from your diet and adopt a high-protein, low-carbohydrate approach to the foods you add to your diet. The low-FODMAP diet is a perfect high-protein, low-carbohydrate diet that can be adopted to reduce symptoms, such as bloating and gas, according to The American College of Gastroenterology. That's because the low-FODMAP diet is relatively low in fats, contains protein-rich foods, and is also quite low in fermentable carbs (FODMAPS), including lactose and fructose. Since the low-FODMAP diet is not a permanent eating plan but rather a diet implemented to treat IBS symptoms, people that have it can, in addition to this book, consult a dietician to set up a diet tailored to gradually integrating certain foods back into your diet after successfully completing the low-FODMAP diet.

Steer clear of meals that contain too much fat

It's not that fat is bad for you, but too much can be quite damaging to your gut and even cause you to experience symptoms, such as diarrhea, particularly in IBS-D patients. That's why it's necessary to limit fats in your diet. IBS diarrhea in IBS-D patients can occur as a symptom every day, causing a person's body to have bowel movements as quickly as 60 minutes after eating a meal, as opposed to individuals with healthy digestive systems that don't have IBS, who only have bowel movements an hour to several hours after they've eaten a meal. With IBS-D patients, vigorous colon contractions occur in individuals and trigger diarrhea and cramping. To improve your digestive response to food, you should avoid eating high-fat meals, especially processed foods, as this triggers your reactive response to having a bowel movement within 60 minutes of consuming food.

Invest in probiotics for your gut health

Probiotics are powerful little helpers for the body and can replenish good sources of bacteria actively living in your gut. It can generally be found as an active culture in yogurt or probiotic powder but can also be taken in the form of capsules. The best way to integrate probiotics into your diet, along with medication or positive dietary alterations, is to start with eating one or two cups of yogurt per day to see how your body responds. Should your body require more probiotics due to the lack of good bacteria in your gut, it is recommended to take prescription capsules to fulfill your needs. Alternatively, you can also sprinkle the powder over your food. Probiotic supplements can also be purchased from pharmacies and don't require a prescription. To establish the dosage your body needs, you can consult with your doctor.

Eat more fiber

Plenty of people lack fiber in their diets, which can cause a range of digestive issues in the body, including not being able to have a bowel movement for a long time. Understanding the anatomy of the human body, it's easy to see why our bodies need to have frequent bowel movements. It is necessary to rid the body of toxins, waste, and allow the body to function optimally. The leading cause of lacking fiber in your diet is constipation, and if you're experiencing it, you should increase your fiber intake. Excellent sources of fiber to include in your diet include beans, cereals, whole-grain bread and grains, vegetables, and fruit. If you're upping your fiber intake but not seeing results, you can request a fiber supplement from your doctor to assist IBS symptoms, such as constipation.

Find out why you have IBS

When you know what caused your condition, then you'll most likely discover how to treat it. In most cases, stress is either the leading or contributing factor to it, including physical, environmental, and emotional stress, all of which can worsen your symptoms. By practicing relaxing strategies, you can possibly reduce IBS symptoms. Yoga or some form of physical exercise practice can help you manage your stress properly. Apart from managing stress and your relationship with food, you can also find out what caused your condition to begin with and track the root of the problem. In some cases, people have experienced trauma, abuse, or psychological damage that can severely affect their symptoms, which is why also seeking counseling is a great way to combat IBS and remain the healthiest version of yourself you can possibly be.

The Benefits of Vagus Nerve Stimulation for the Digestive System

mens sana in corpore sano

The vagus nerve is a primary component responsible for the parasympathetic nervous system, which is also in charge of many bodily functions, including your immune system response, heart rate, **digestion**, and the ability to have control over your mood, which affects the state of your mental health. Most importantly of all, it is responsible for the connections and communication between the brain, which relays necessary information to the gastrointestinal tract. This information includes the health of inner organs in the body, in direct relation to the brain, and gets transported with the help of afferent fibers.

Although there are many different types of nerves in the body performing important individual functions, the vagus nerve does more than communicate with our gastrointestinal tract to ensure the correct messages are translated. It also treats disorders of the gastrointestinal tract, along with psychiatric disorders. Needless to say, if your vagus nerve is not working properly, it can result in a hostile environment in which bodily functions will be left impaired and unable to thrive as it should.

Evidence suggests that the stimulation of the vagus nerve is an add-on treatment option that has shown positive results, especially because it can treat posttraumatic stress disorder, treatment-refractory depression, as well as inflammatory bowel disease. Vagus nerve stimulation acts as the ideal treatment to amplify and improve vagal tone, which also increases the production of cytokine, which aids as a crucial mechanism to build up a sense of resilience in the body.

With vagus nerve stimulation, the vagal afferent fibers present in the gut have the ability to affect monoaminergic brain systems located in the brain stem, which positively affects vagus nerve activity. With stimulation, the nerve can normalize responses to stress in the brain, ultimately preventing sending stress responses to the gastrointestinal tract. Stimulation can be induced through breathing, particularly adding meditation or exercise practices to your daily routine, which can additionally prevent anxiety and boost your mood, promoting an overall healthy mind-to-body experience.

Given the important role of the vagus nerve in the body, stimulating it can present many systems, such as the gastrointestinal tract, with many benefits by simply allowing for proper communication between the brain and digestive system. Consistent stimulation of the vagus nerve can thus do wonders for the adequate function of gastrointestinal organs and prevent disorders such as irritable bowel syndrome (IBS), irritable bowel dysfunction (IBD), Crohn's disease, and inflammatory bowel disease.

Vagus nerve stimulation can recover a low vagal tone index, the main cause of vagus nerve dysfunction that results in psychological and digestive disorders.

How to increase the vagus nerve stimulation:

Deep breathing

About yoga, one of the most effective ways to stimulate your vagus nerve is by taking deep breaths and slowing down your respiration rate. Typically, we take between 9 -13 breaths per minute. To stimulate your vagus nerve, you can slow this down to 6 breaths per minute by:

- Inhaling slowly to a count of 6

- Exhaling slowly to a count of 6

- Repeat this rhythm until you feel a sense of calmness.

Deep and slow breathing techniques are effective in slowing down your heart rate. They also act to stimulate your vagus nerve to release Acetylcholine, which is a powerful parasympathetic neurotransmitter that aids in calming the body and restoring it to a rested and relaxed state.

When you feel anxious or stressed out, try this simple breathing technique, and you will be amazed at how effective it is in soothing you into a calm and relaxed state. When the body is in a rested state, psychological and physical health is boosted.

Expose yourself to Cold therapy

Cholinergic neurons present in the vagus nerve are activated by exposure to cold. This makes exposing yourself to cold temperatures an easy and effective way to stimulate vagal tone or activity. The cold temperature effectively inhibits the sympathetic responses of fight or flight.

To use cold therapy to activate your vagus nerve, there are various techniques you can use. For example, you can simply turn the water to cold for the last two minutes of your regular shower. Alternatively, splashing ice-cold water on your face will also have a positive effect on your vagus nerve. Taking a walk outside when the temperature is low can also help you activate the vagus nerve.

If you feel that your body is up for the challenge, you can also try taking ice baths. This will involve putting three bags of ice into a half-filled tub and getting in once the ice is melted. To do this safely, ensure that you do not stay in the ice bath for an extended period of time. Taking a hot beverage after the ice bath will be effective in warming you up again.

Cold temperatures have been found to have an effect on reducing stress, anxiety, and **stimulating the gastric nerves** through vagal stimulation. When you feel yourself getting anxious, losing concentration, or simply getting worn out mentally, splash some cold water on your face or just take a break and walk outside in the cold for a while; it may not solve your problem, but it will definitely calm you down and clear your mind.

Diet

The Vagus nerve is surrounded by a protective sheath of myelin that protects the vagus nerve from injury and ensures that nerve impulses are transmitted properly. Good myelin health is, therefore, important for the proper function of your Vagus nerve.

The health of the myelin sheath, however, starts to deteriorate as we age, meaning that the vagus nerve becomes more susceptible to injury and malfunction the older we get. This protective layer, myelin, is a lipid-based compound, and we can help mitigate the effects of aging on the myelin by observing a healthy diet which should be characterized by;

- **Healthy fats:** Myelin sheath is made up of a fatty layer. This means that eating healthy fats is a good way to keep the myelin around the nerves intact and in good condition. Healthy fats are fats that have good cholesterol such as olive oil, omega 3 fatty acids from fatty fish, and oils from seeds and nuts such as chia seeds.

- **Vitamin C**: This essential vitamin plays a major role in the formation of myelin and enhances the formation of neurons that improve brain function. A diet rich in Vitamin C will, therefore, go a long way in improving your nervous function by ensuring that the vagus nerve is well protected by the myelin sheath.
Fruits such as **strawberries, kiwis, oranges, guavas (ripe), papayas, and lemons are great sources of vitamin C.** That you can incorporate into your diet. Vegetables such as **broccoli, brussels sprouts, bell peppers, and kale** are also rich in vitamin C, but the beast vegetable with this vitamin is **savoy cabbage**.

- **Reduce alcohol consumption**: It is no secret that excessive alcohol consumption impacts brain function. This is partly because alcohol contributes to the degradation of the myelin sheath that protects cranial nerves, including the vagus nerve.

Intermittent fasting

Intermittent fasting refers to a nutrition plan where you eat for a certain period of time, followed by a period of abstaining from food, which is the fasting phase. Intermittent fasting means fasting in intervals. For example, you can fast for 18 hours in a day and restrict your feeding period to 6 hours.

When you fast, the vagus nerve detects the inevitable drop that occurs in glucose levels when we go without eating. Once it has detected the drop in blood glucose, the vagus nerve signals the brain to reduce metabolism, which has the effect of slowing down the heart rate and switching of the body's sympathetic responses of fight or flight. In this way, fasting is effective in stimulating vagal activity.

Intermittent fasting has become one of the more popular weight loss methods because it is effective in insulin regulation, and therefore, promotes fat burning in the body. This method, apart from the obvious benefits in terms of weight management, is an effective way to activate the vagus nerve.

If you are trying this method for the first time, an easy tip to incorporate to avoid suffering from hunger pangs is to make your sleeping hours part of your fasting window. For example, you can opt to have your fasting window from 7 pm in the evening to noon the next day, so that most of the fasting period will be used up while you sleep; this means that you will not need to experience hunger throughout the day.

Another great hack for intermittent fasting is ensuring that during the eating window, you consume a lot of proteins as opposed to carbohydrates. This will aid you during the fasting period because proteins are effective as an appetite suppressant; in the low FODMAP diet the foods with the best protein content are unprocessed fish and meat. Reducing your carbohydrate intake will also be effective in reducing the blood sugar fluctuations that typically occur between the fasting period and the eating window. Water and non-caloric drinks such as green tea is also a great way to stay hydrated and curb hunger pangs during the fasting window.

To benefit from the effects of fasting in stimulating your vagus nerve, you can opt for moderate fasting plans of 16 hours or 18 hours a couple of times in a week. The ultimate effect is that fasting by stimulating your vagus nerve will also have positive effects on your mental clarity and digestive processes to relief IBS.

Physical Exercise

There is no getting away from the fact that physical exercise has multiple beneficial effects on our physical health. It not only improves cardiovascular health; it also helps in fat burning and weight management. Exercise has also been proven to be effective in combating stress and anxiety. When we engage in physical exercise, the body release chemicals called endorphins that have an uplifting effect on the mood and are responsible for the feel-good after effect of exercising.

If that's not enough to get you up and moving, physical exercise is an effective way to stimulate your vagus nerve and enhance your vagal tone. Exercise stimulates your vagus nerve resulting in enhanced mental clarity and stimulation of the brain's growth hormone.

Exercise is a good way to manage stress and boost your immune system. Physical activity stimulates brain function, making you more alert and enhances digestive processes by boosting metabolism and stimulates the movement of food along the digestive tract.

When it comes to stimulating the vagus nerve using physical exercise, there is no limit to the type of exercises you can use. Lifting weights, jogging, taking brisk walks, aerobics, and even yoga will all help in boosting vagal activity and promoting the body's self-healing mechanisms.

To learn specific exercises to activate vagus nerve you should read my other book titled: *'Vagus Nerve Secrets'*

In this book you can find simple exercises exercises suitable for all ages and you can make at home and without weights or other equipment!

Massage

Massages can be so relaxing and effective in relieving tension and stress in the body. It is, therefore, no surprise that they can be used as a means of activating the vagus nerve. One of the most effective massages when it comes to vagal activation is reflexology massages.

A reflexology massage involves the application of different amounts of pressure to different parts of the body, specifically, the feet, hands, and ears. A reflexology massage will increase the activity of the vagus nerve, inhibit sympathetic fight or flight responses and even slow down the heart rate. This means that this type of massages soothes the body into a relaxed state that promotes vagal function and mental clarity.

Massaging the neck area is also effective in stimulating the vagus nerve by applying pressure on the carotid sinus. Pressure massages are also effective in vagal stimulation. When you are feeling tense or having a bad day, visiting a good massage therapist will help you to relax and reduce your anxiety and stress levels.

Sleep on the right side of your body

You're probably wondering how sleeping on the right or left side of your body has anything to do with stimulating nerves in your brain, but lying on your back actually decreases your vagus nerve activation, which can be harmful to the body. Sleeping on the right side of your body, however, boosts vagus nerve stimulation, as opposed to sleeping on the left side, which doesn't increase or decrease the vagus nerve whatsoever.

The Importance of the Vagus Nerve

The vagus nerve recognizes and fights off inflammation in the body, which is why it is crucial for maintaining a pathogen-free environment inside of the body.

Stimulation of the vagus nerve fights off inflammation, which is, without doubt, the underlying cause of most diseases people deal with every day. It attacks the immune system, which activates an inflammatory response that protects cells against potential danger, which is the point when your body generally starts acting up, displaying symptoms of possible issues you may be experiencing internally. Since the vagus nerve is responsible for recognizing potential threats, such as inflammation in the body, it prepares the immune system to send out a stress response to the brain, which also alerts us when we are not feeling well or in this case, **experiencing IBS** or other gastrointestinal disorder symptoms. In that same breath, one can also say that the vagus nerve protects the body from developing even worse conditions, as the presence of symptoms usually warn us about underlying issues we may experience with our bodies.

The vagus nerve is important and is responsible for many operational functions in the body and extends from the brainstem and cerebellum throughout the body, branching out into major organs to support the proper functioning of it. Organs that rely on the vagus nerve include the larynx, heart, esophagus, the pharynx, stomach, small intestine, as well as the large intestine. Extending from the brain throughout the body, the vagus nerve is responsible for senses and functions, such as taste, smell, swallowing, heart rate, speech, excretion, and proper digestion. It is thus a very important nerve in the brain that cannot be compromised. As the benefits of vagus nerve stimulation are listed above, it is quite easy to stimulate the vagus nerve and ensure it is functioning optimally. In a nutshell, living a healthy life that is filled with healthy food, exercise, habits, and respecting your body really makes a difference in what will carry you through life, as well as how well you live in the next decades of your life.

Eating a healthy diet and following healthy habits is not about losing weight, but it's about something much more than that.

Most people, for instance, have never even heard of the vagus nerve and how important it is to keep it in good health, yet it's so essential for the functioning of your body. This proves once more why you are what you eat and how you can dictate your own health by living better every day.

The vagus nerve is also crucial to the body's parasympathetic nervous system (PNS) and cannot be replaced, which is why it should be treated with respect. It plays a role in many physiological activities, also known as, "rest and digest." Since the PNS is responsible for keeping the body in a calm state and digesting food accordingly, with the purpose to rejuvenate the body and restore its energy supply, any supporting mechanism of the PNS is essential for maintaining a healthy body.

To fulfill its functions in the body, the vagus nerve also communicates with organs by simply releasing a very important neurotransmitter, acetylcholine, which is responsible for regulating blood pressure regulation, heart rate, digestion, sweating, blood glucose balance, taste, breathing, kidney function, crying, saliva secretion, bile release, and orgasms, and female fertility. Given its long list of responsibilities in the body, it also communicates with hormones to ensure all bodily functions are performed effectively. Hormones, such as insulin, are responsible for decreasing the release of glucose from the liver with the purpose to stimulate the vagus nerve, while T3, a thyroid hormone, activates vagus nerve stimulation to ensure appetite is increased when needed, along with the production of ghrelin, a function responsible for increasing hunger in the body.

Finally, proper functioning of the vagus nerve is very important to release oxytocin, vasoactive intestinal peptide, and testosterone, all of which play a role in producing the growth hormone GHRH, as well as activating the parathyroid hormone, which is used to convert vitamin D3 to activated vitamin D.

The vagus nerve has a massive impact on one's mental and physical health. Since it affects the brain, spinal cord, hormones, and countless functions in the body that are necessary for us to survive, it is incredibly important to maintain proper and healthy functioning of the vagal tone index.

6 Practices to Stimulate the Vagus Nerve

1 Slow rhythmic and diaphragmatic breathing

This exercise can be achieved by breathing from your diaphragm deeply instead of engaging in taking shallow breaths from the top of your lungs, which most people tend to do. By breathing deeply from your diaphragm, you can increase the vagus nerve stimulation.

2 Practice yoga

Meditation? Yes, it is a wonderful way to recover both the mind and body from various things, particularly any imbalance or lack of harmony in the body. Yoga is one of the biggest and most helpful forms of meditation that raises your serotonin levels and lowers anxiety. It can also increase the effectiveness of the vagus nerve, as well as treat the parasympathetic system's activity, ensuring it works properly.

Yoga is one of the best treatment options for vagus nerve stimulation due to it being a slow, deep breathing practice, which activates the sensitive pressure receptors of the heart, neck, and spine, allowing baroreceptors to send messages to the brain, which then instructs it to activate the vagus nerve.

3 Humming

Just like speaking, humming can be achieved due to its connectivity to the vocal cords, which mechanically stimulates the vagus nerves. By simply humming a song or repeating the sound "OM" several times per exercise, you can improve your vagal tone.

4 Meditation practices

Meditation, in general, can improve vagus nerve stimulation, but any practice focused on love and kindness can promote possible feelings of goodwill, which transcends from yourself to others. This can increase positive emotions immediately, which increases social closeness to others, an improved relationship with yourself, and even improved vagal tone.

5 Balance your gut microbiome

This can be achieved by adding more healthy bacteria to your gut, which creates positive feedback that translates back to your vagus nerve, essentially increasing its vagal tone.

6 Wash your face with cold water

By washing your face with cold water once or twice a day, the cold sensation on your face can stimulate your vagus nerve, which is an easy way to stimulate it daily.

If you want learn more about meditation techniques, I wrote an entire chapter about this in my book:

'Vagus Nerve Secrets'.

How to Recognize Vagus Nerve Dysfunction

The vagus nerve extends through many areas in the body, which could potentially cause various parts of it to become dysfunctional if the vagus nerve doesn't work properly. Dysfunction of the vagus nerve can affect three main areas, all of which are responsible for the functioning of the entire body. These include brain communication, brain-to-organ communication, and organ-to-brain communication. If any of these areas are dysfunctional, it could cause the body to react in many ways, including chronic inflammation, dizziness, fainting, heartburn, aggression, anxiety, delayed stomach emptying, brain fog, depression, fatigue, heartburn, a heart rate that changes too rapidly, weight gain, difficulty swallowing, vitamin B12 deficiency, and most relevant to this guide, IBS.

When dysfunction of the vagus nerve is left untreated, it is possible for a range of serious diseases to occur in the body, the cause of which is often misdiagnosed by medical professionals. It can escalate to the point where one can develop serious diseases, such as autism, chronic heart failure, alcohol addiction, bulimia, fibromyalgia, migraines, cancer, leaky gut syndrome, mood disorders, memory disorders, such as dementia or Alzheimer's disease, obesity, tinnitus, multiple sclerosis, poor blood circulation, and obsessive-compulsive disorder (OCD).

To prevent potentially getting diseases, the vagus nerve must be protected, which can only be done when your lifestyle choices and health habits are in check. By keeping yourself as healthy as you can, you can also reduce the chances of suffering from symptoms, such as alcoholism, fatigue, stress, diabetes, impaired posture, and possible damage to the vagus nerve.

By adopting the low-FODMAP diet, in addition to adjusting your lifestyle and incorporating ways to stimulate the vagus nerve, you could become the healthiest version of yourself possible. With your vagus nerve in check, you can also improve the management of your condition, IBS, or any other related digestive and intestinal tract disorders. It's important to keep in mind that without the proper functioning of the vagus nerve, your body cannot thrive optimally. The vagus nerve is also discussed more in detail in my previous book,

Vagus Nerve Secrets, where you can learn more about how to treat the vagus nerve to relieve different issues and potential current or future health concerns in your body.

How to Follow the Low-FODMAP Diet

Irritable bowel syndrome is a very serious gastrointestinal condition that is characterized by its symptoms, all of which are related to the disruption of the proper functioning of the digestive system.

Based on all you've learned about IBS, gastrointestinal conditions as a whole, the digestive system, and particularly, the low-FODMAP diet in this guide, starting the diet for yourself is a positive step in the right direction for managing your symptoms and getting your health back on track.

Yes, after testing positive for IBS, you can visit your doctor and get prescription medication to treat your condition, but without following a proper diet to support your current state of health and alleviate your symptoms, you won't be able to heal your body from the inside out as necessary. The low-FODMAP is perfect for getting rid of your symptoms. If you integrate it, including all its rules, into your diet, you will learn what's good for your body and what's not.

The diet is designed to bring people with IBS almost instant relief from painful and uncomfortable symptoms while treating the condition accordingly. After you've been diagnosed with IBS, or perhaps even a related digestive disorder, it's extremely important to gather the correct information on how to treat your condition in the best possible way you can. Although hearing that you've been diagnosed with something as serious as a lifelong condition, such as IBS, is never easy, it's certainly something that needs to be taken seriously and requires treatment to improve the quality of your life. Since IBS plays a major role in disrupting the quality of one's life, accompanied by pain and discomfort, it is necessary to manage it in the best way you possibly can.

The low-FODMAP diet can be broken down into six structured phases to get you started and help you combat the symptoms of IBS successfully.

Steps include:

1. Consultation
2. Reflection and Initiation
3. Planning and Execution
4. High-FODMAPs elimination
5. High-FODMAPs reintroduction
6. Diet and lifestyle personalization

Phase 1: Dietary Consultation

The most important thing to take into consideration after you've been diagnosed with IBS is that it can be treated, your symptoms can be relieved, and you can live an improved lifestyle and maintain a sense of normal living without having to worry about your condition. This is advice even your doctor should be able to tell you, and while he/she will be quick to prescribe you with the medication necessary to relieve pain or treat your symptoms, apart from supplements, medication isn't always the best medicine to treat your condition. Seeking answers from a dietician, somebody who has extensive knowledge of the digestive system and how foods affect it, along with its disorders, is the best way to go.

Both doctors and dieticians prescribe the low-FODMAP diet as the best option to deal with gastrointestinal tract disorders. Your dietician may even emphasize how serious it is to adopt the diet's rules in your daily life. A dietician will also prescribe a range of other different forms of self-healing to accommodate your diet, including anything that could possibly stimulate the vagus nerve, such as exercise, meditation, counseling, massage therapy, acupuncture, etc. However, any additional measures you take to treat your condition is entirely up to you, based on what you believe to be adequate to integrate into your daily routine.

Consulting a dietician to guide you on your low-FODMAP journey, even after you've completed six weeks of the diet, can be beneficial to managing your condition long-term. If you're not aware of any respectable dieticians, you could ask your doctor to refer you to one that specializes in IBS. Apart from assisting you on your diet, a dietician can tell you what types of low-FODMAP foods to eat and which to avoid (high-FODMAPS). He/she will also keep track of your progress to see whether your body is reacting negatively to any specific types of foods more than it should. The goal of integrating low-FODMAP foods into your diet should be to combat symptoms and make you feel better while also learning what works for your body.

Starting with any diet, it is important to recognize that food serves as fuel for our bodies and that when it reacts to certain types of food, such as gluten, dairy, or sugars differently than what it should, it happens for a reason and is not welcomed by our bodies. Although it can seem difficult to decrease the intake, or perhaps cut out foods from your diet completely for six weeks, it gets easier when you understand why you're doing it and also adopting a positive and prospective mindset as to why you're doing it. A dietician will also push you to focus on the image of yourself after you've completed the six-week low-FODMAP diet. Starting, you can consider how much better you feel after just one week of following the diet, and as you progress in the next few weeks, reflect on all the symptoms that have been relieved on your low-FODMAP journey.

Eating the right types of food isn't a punishment for your body but rather a means of showing respect for it. Dieticians will consult your doctor to check whether you can proceed with the low-FODMAP diet and consider your health, current habits, and health-related goals you'd like to achieve.

Before starting the low-FODMAP diet, know that:

- You can achieve amazing results when you consult a dietary professional who is educated and trained to create diet plans for IBS patients.

- The purpose of the low-FODMAP diet is not to limit the types of food you consume, but instead, increase the different types you add into your diet. Eating a wide variety of food is necessary to support all your body's nutritional requirements, and much like increasing your fiber intake (recommended), also improving your immune system and symptoms as a result.

- Having a support system, such as a dietary consultant or fitness coach once you embark on your journey to restore your health and find the best possible way to manage your condition, you'll be able to adopt a new, healthier lifestyle far more easily than you would otherwise.

- Dieticians can assist you by identifying all the foods and nutritional sources responsible for creating a disruptive environment inside your body.

- Dieticians who specialize in IBS are trained to identify different FODMAPs and the effects they have on the body, which will allow them to easily assist you and help you to adjust your daily meals to eventually completely prevent your symptoms from occurring.

- IBS isn't a curable condition, only a treatable one, which is why it is necessary to understand it. Knowing that you can improve it, and improve it to a point that you won't even recognize you're living with it, can be achieved.

- 86% of individuals diagnosed with IBS experienced their symptoms improving after adopting the low-FODMAP diet.

- The diet is also highly recommended for people living with Crohn's disease, SIBO, dysfunctional gastrointestinal disorders, and colitis.

Phase 2: Reflection and Consideration

Finding out you have a disorder or disease that will last you a lifetime is quite scary at first. Once you find out what it is you're dealing with and how to overcome the pitfalls of it, the journey gets a whole lot better. Before starting the low-FODMAP diet, it's necessary to take time and reflect on all the reasons why you're doing it. Imagining how much you could potentially gain from it is a great way to get yourself to change your lifestyle, and not only for the six-week duration of the diet but for the rest of your life. Coming to terms with the fact that you are living with IBS and considering the reason why you're changing or improving different aspects of your lifestyle can help you overcome lack of motivation, your symptoms, along with challenges you may face on the road ahead.

With IBS, the great hope is that you can always improve your health and lifestyle, which will reflect on the outcome of your disorder or disease.

Just because you are living with IBS doesn't necessarily mean it has to feel like it.

You are in control of the outcome of your health.

What to consider before starting the low-FODMAP diet:

Never start a new diet before consulting your doctor and dietary expert

Given that the low-FODMAP diet is incredibly limiting, the best thing you could possibly do is seek both medical and nutritional advice from professionals. IBS is a condition that can worsen if not treated properly, and since it's easy to cut out foods from your diet, you do risk not consuming the necessary nutrients required to sustain your health, daily nutrition, and dietary needs, as well as your energy levels.

Take note of all nutritional labels

If you're not used to reading the nutrition labels on packaging, then you're definitely going to be in for a treat as you'll have to start reading them whenever you buy, eat, or drink something. If you didn't think the low-FODMAP is a strict diet, think again. Although you are permitted to eat a very low quantity of high-FODMAP foods, it poses as a major adjustment for those who are used to eating wholewheat carbohydrates, starches, flour-based foods, etc. Following the diet, it is necessary to read product labels carefully as many packaged foods contain long lists of ingredients. You should also take into consideration that, if you don't know what an ingredient is, you probably shouldn't be eating the product. Keeping track of high-FODMAP foods are also quite intense as it includes a long list of foods you must exclude from your diet, which is quite a difficult task when you're shopping for food. That's why it's important to know what you're allowed to eat, and what you're not.

You'll have to consider adding new foods and sources of nutrients to your daily diet, even some that you may be reluctant to try

Since the low-FODMAP diet is all about adding variety to your diet, you must consider the possibility of adding new foods to your diet, along with a wide range of different foods, including a range of vegetables. Many people don't like vegetables, which is thought to be something you can learn to like over time. There are also countless new ways to, so to say, "spice up your meals," which includes herbs, spices, dressings, and oils. Adding these essential ingredients to your meals is a great way to amplify your meals. Herbs and spices are especially two incredible sources you can use to amplify the taste of your meals, as it can make nearly anything taste better.

When in doubt, add a dash of hummus to all of the foods you don't like.

Don't confuse the low-FODMAP diet for a dairy-free or gluten-free diet

There are many people who love gluten and dairy and can't stand the idea of quitting it altogether. Now, if you're dairy-intolerant or gluten-intolerant, you should listen to your body and quit the culprits altogether, but if you're not and you're living with IBS, there's no need to worry about having to quit delicious sources of dairy or gluten altogether. The low-FODMAP diet doesn't condone cutting out any type of food. Instead, it just manages the quantity that you're allowed to consume. A gluten-free or dairy-free diet should not be confused with the low-FODMAP diet. As an example, even the low-FODMAP diet excludes most gluten-based products from the diet, but it does allow you to eat sourdough spelt bread as a low-gluten-based option.

Be careful when choosing your condiments

Although salad dressings are heaven-sent to improve the taste of food on your plate, most types thereof aren't recommended on the low-FODMAP diet. In fact, most salad dressings, salsa, ketchup, and spice mixtures all contain high-FODMAPs, such as garlic, onion, honey, and the worst of all, high-fructose corn syrup. Yes, you read correctly, garlic and onions are high-FODMAP foods.

Queue the violin music... It's going to be okay.

Vegetables are important, but...

Everyone is aware by now, but the low-FODMAP diet actually recommends you to exclude vegetables such as onions and garlic, asparagus, cauliflower, mushrooms, scallions, spring onions, and peas from your diet. You're also only allowed to eat extremely small quantities of mangoes, pears, raisins, plums, peaches, sultanas, raisins, watermelon, avocados, ripe bananas, apricots, apples, grapefruit, and blackberries. Although this list may seem extreme, it is necessary to follow to avoid potential disruptive reactions from occurring in your digestive tract.

You can still drink some types of alcohol

Alcohol isn't recommended for people living with most

gastrointestinal disorders, yet you are allowed to drink vodka, whiskey, and even beer while following a low-FODMAP diet. However, in the spirit of making good choices for your body, it's best to mix vodka or whiskey with soda water instead of mixers, as most contain fructose, which is considered a high-FODMAP ingredient.

Getting discouraged on the low-FODMAP diet shouldn't be an option

While one person may find the low-FODMAP diet to be incredibly easy, others may find it to be very difficult. Nevertheless, there is hope in the sense that the low-FODMAP diet only lasts six weeks, which is followed by a better-maintained balance of low-FODMAPs vs. high-FODMAPS. It means that the low-FODMAP diet serves as a mere basis or introduction to living a healthier lifestyle, which is something everybody should be doing, regardless of whether they are diagnosed with IBS, IBD, colitis, Crohn's disease, or any other temporary or permanent gastrointestinal disorder.

The low-FODMAP diet may present itself as difficult to follow

This diet is considered one of the most difficult diets to follow and requires an adaptation of learning how to cook with only certain types of food.

If you're overwhelmed by it, take a step back and consider the benefits again. When you know why you're doing what you're doing and you have a purposeful goal, it will be easier to follow through. If you feel overwhelmed, gather up some family or friends and tell them about your diagnosis and why you've chosen to follow the diet. Discuss the benefits and struggles you experience with it, ask them to support you, and follow up phase two with phase three, planning your low-FODMAP journey before starting it.

Phase 3: Planning and Execution

After you've consulted with your doctor and a dietician, and they've given you the green light to continue with the low-FODMAP diet, you can decide when it's the right time to start. Of course, starting immediately is recommended because it can significantly reduce the effects that IBS symptoms have on the body. But some people may require more time to prepare themselves mentally before starting the diet. Others need a while to plan everything before executing it.

The low-FODMAP diet is a serious endeavor, one that is difficult to start and maintain, which is also why people sometimes opt for trying it out for two weeks at a time. Typically, you can adopt the low-FODMAP diet for two to six weeks, which includes the elimination phase, followed by the high-FODMAP reintroduction phase (phase 5), which typically lasts between six and eight weeks, depending on your preference. It is a challenge and can be designated as a goal in your life. You can literally add it to your checklist of things you need to get done in a certain period and reward yourself after you've completed it.

Adjusting your daily eating habits isn't easy, but it can become quite enjoyable if you approach it in a positive way. There are countless recipes to be found online that can turn your low-FODMAP diet journey into a delicious and maintainable one.

To maintain your diet, it is recommended to keep a food diary, and journal in detail daily. Pin down the foods you're planning on incorporating into your diet each week so that you can find a way to balance out your meals, avoid consuming large quantities of high-FODMAPs, and ensure you manage to consume all the nutrients necessary to maintain your optimal health. It is necessary to plan this, especially because the low-FODMAP diet eliminates high-FODMAP foods from your diet, which may be a source of necessary nutrients.

Writing down everything you'll be eating the following day or entire week is helpful to keep you on top of your game, avoiding the opportunity to eat something you shouldn't or snacking unnecessarily. When you write down the meals you have to plan for, including the groceries you'll need to shop for to make them, you are taking a moment to care about what you're putting in your body. It allows for a conscious moment of reflection about the reason why you've decided to follow the low-FODMAP diet. It also presents you with a greater understanding to learn more about the relationship between all the types of food you eat, along with possible symptoms you may experience.

A great test for yourself before you start the low-FODMAP diet is to write down your current diet for a week and follow it accordingly. Then, at the end of each day or two hours after eating each meal, write down how that meal made you feel. If you detect a pattern of feeling bloated, experiencing stomach pain, gas or feeling uncomfortable, you can recognize what types of high-FODMAPs are responsible for sensitivity responses in your gastrointestinal tract. Writing down your meals when starting the low-FODMAP diet will also aid in the discovery of the foods you can eat that don't affect your body in a negative way and those that you should avoid.

Keeping track of your meals every day has also been linked to weight loss and can reduce stress, anxiety, and depression. Since journalling is a mindful act of care for the mind, and adopting a diet to support your health journey is an act of care for the body, it can benefit your mental wellbeing, which can also translate into physical wellness.

After planning your week or even pre-planning two to six weeks of the low-FODMAP diet and writing down a grocery list, you can turn your plans into action and buy everything you need to start your first week of the diet. It is recommended to set a day in the week that suits your schedule best and treat it like an errand or chore you have to do each week to ensure you don't run out of pre-planned meal ingredients or succumb to opting for high-FODMAP foods.

Once you've completed your weekly grocery haul, you can choose to prep meals or cook them fresh every day. Organizing your fridge and pantry is also a great way to stay inspired throughout the week to follow your goals. It is also very important to choose meals that work for you and not just meals that comply with the low-FODMAP diet's guidelines. If you're not enjoying your meals, you probably won't stick to the diet, which is something that needs to be addressed and eliminated from the start. A great way to stay intrigued in the diet is to take meals you love and find ways to continue eating them but modifying them low-FODMAP style. An example is cooking mac and cheese but without the macaroni pasta and the cheddar cheese. Instead, you can replace the macaroni pasta with spiralized zucchini noodles, and the cheese with nutritional yeast. The end result is a vegan meal that tastes exactly the same as traditional mac and cheese. Before embarking on the actual diet, you can play around with recipes. If your dietician has recommended possible recipes or a structured meal plan, you can find ways of adjusting the recommended meals too and swap out ingredients according to your preference.

Over-planning and getting excited about cooking new meals is much better than not planning at all and struggling to stick to a new diet, which is both difficult for most individuals to follow. Online blogs, cooking shows, and even YouTube can present you with enough inspiration to last you a lifetime.

If you're into technology, you can also download apps to support your journey. Applications such as Fast FODMAP, Kitchen Stories, Cara, Bowelle, Symple, Fast Tract, and Deliciously Ella are just a few apps you can download on your iOS or Android smart devices that can simplify your experience and keep you motivated on the low-FODMAP diet.

It only takes a little bit of innovation every day to embrace the worthwhileness of what it is you're actually doing for your health.

Phase 4: High-FODMAPs Elimination

Learning about the low-FODMAP diet, you've probably never considered that food can have such an adverse range of effects on your body. Once you are diagnosed with IBS or any other related digestive disorder, you may feel discouraged or like you'd give anything to get rid of the symptoms you're experiencing as a result of your condition. Luckily, the low-FODMAP diet presents you with an option to combat your daily struggles with IBS, and with guidance from this *Low-FODMAP Diet for Beginners*, you've finally been introduced to the possibilities of the diet and what it can do for you.

Following the dietary consultation, reflection and consideration, and planning and execution phases, phase 4 presents a very important step of eliminating sources of high-FODMAPs in your diet, all of which have probably contributed to your condition and worsening symptoms.

The elimination phase is a crucial step in the low-FODMAP diet, along with the high-FODMAP reintroduction phase, and will help you bridge the terrain of actually switching from your current eating habits to ones best suited for your body, and finally, reintroducing a common balance between low-FODMAPs and high-FODMAPS to create a more sustainable diet.

High-FODMAP foods include the following:

- Fructans, present in certain fruits, nuts, grains, and vegetables

- Fructose, present in certain fruits

- Lactose, present in certain dairy products

- GOS, present in beans, lentils, and chickpeas

- Polyols, present in certain fruits, artificial sweeteners, and vegetables

Understanding the elimination phase, it's necessary to know that the term "elimination phase" doesn't mean completely eliminating high-FODMAPs from your diet but rather reducing it to a point that it cannot affect your body or eliminating it entirely to see whether your health and symptoms improve. Since the low-FODMAP diet is only two to six weeks in duration, the point of the elimination phase is to dramatically reduce high-FODMAPs in your diet, all of which potentially causes your body to have a sensitivity reaction to them. The outcome of the diet should present you with a better understanding of how to control your symptoms.

During the elimination phase, you will learn how your body feels without certain FODMAPS to maximize the level control you have over your symptoms. It will also allow you to discover factors that can possibly contribute to IBS symptoms, as well as how to manage them, and finally, present your body with a clean slate to adjust your eating habits and lifestyle. This phase is important to confirm whether you are FODMAP-sensitive or alternatively, suffering from colonic hypersensitivity. Apart from learning about your condition and how to treat it, you can also learn about your body, which can improve your energy levels, boost your mood, and wellness daily.

To carry out the elimination phase successfully, you must be able to distinguish between low-FODMAPs and high-FODMAPs.

FOOD LISTS

FRUITS

Allowed	Allowed in limited quantities	Avoid
BANANA (unripe)	AVOCADO	APPLES
BLUEBERRIES	BANANA (RIPE)	APRICOTS
CHESTNUTS	COCONUT	BLACKBERRIES
CLEMENTINE	POMEGRANATE	CHERRIES
CRANBERRY		FIGS
GRAPES		GRAPEFRUIT
GUAVA (RIPE)		MANGO
KIWI		PEACHES
LEMONS		PEARS
LIME		PERSIMMONS
LITCHI		PLUMS
MANDARINS		WATERMELON
MARACUJA (PASSION FRUIT)		
MELON (CANTALOUPE)		
MELON (HONETDEW)		
ORANGES		
PAPAYA		
PINEAPPLE		
PITAYA (DRAGON'S FRUIT)		
PLATANO		
PRICKLY PEARS		
RASPBERRIES		
RHUBARB		
STRAWBERRIES		
TANGERINE		

Scan QR code to download this list

VEGETABLES

Allowed	Allowed in limited quantities	Avoid
ALGAE	ARTICHOKE HEARTS (canned)	ARTICHOKES
AROMATIC HERB (ALL)	BUTTERNUT SQUASH	ASPARAGUS
AUBERGINES	CELERY	**BEANS**: black, broad, kidney, lima, soya
BAMBOO SHOOTS	CORN (canned)	CAULIFLOWER
BELGIAN ENDIVE	DRIED TOMATOES (canned)	GARLIC
BROCCOLI	MUSHROOMS (canned)	JERUSALEM ARTICHOKE
BRUSSELS SPROUTS	RED BEETROOT	LEEKS
CABBAGE	SAVOY CABBAGE	MUSHROOMS
CABBAGE BLACK	SNOW PEAS	ONION
CAPERS	SWEET POTATOES	SCALLIONS
CARROTS		SPRING ONION (white part)
CELERIAC		
CHARD		
CHERRY TOMATOES		
CHICORY LEAVES		
CHINESE CABBAGE		
COURGETTE		
CUCUMBER		
EGGPLANT		
FENNEL		
GINGER		
GREEN BEANS		
ICEBERG LETTUCE		

Allowed
KALE
LETTUCE
NAPA CABBAGE
OKRA
OLIVES
PALMITO
PARSNIP
PEPPERS
POTATOES
PUMPKIN
RADICCHIO
RADISHES
RED CABBAGE
RED PEPPERONI
ROCKET SALAD
SCAROLE
SOY SHOOTS
SPINACH
SPRING ONION (green part)
TOMATOES
TURNIP
WATER CHESTNUT
ZUCCHINI

CEREALS AND FLOURS

Allowed	Allowed in limited quantities	Avoid
Pasta, bread, crackers and other products made only with the following flours:		
BUCKWHEAT (HULLED)	BREAD GLUTEN FREE	AMARANTH FLOUR
CORN	AMARANTH (puffed)	BARLEY
MILE	CORN FLAKES (with gluten)	KAMUT
OATS	OAT FLAKES, INSTANT (pre-cooked)	LUPINE FLOUR
QUINOA	PASTA GLUTEN FREE	RYE
RICE	RICE AND CORN COUS COUS	SPELT
SORGHUM		WHEAT
TAPIOCA		
TEFF		
POTATO STARCH		

DAIRY PRODUCT

Allowed	Allowed in limited quantities	Avoid
ALL VERY AGED CHEESES: Brie, Camembert, Cheddar, Chèvre, Emmental, Feta, Milk flakes, Mozzarella, Parmigiano Reggiano, Pecorino	RICOTTA	**ALL SOFT CHEESES:** mascarpone, Philadelphia, etc
BUTTER MILK (lactose-free) ICE-CREAM (lactose-free) YOGURT (lactose-free) YOGURT (goat)	HALLOUMI	BUTTERMILK CREAM CUSTARD ICE-CREAM (with lactose) KEFIR MILK (cow, goat, sheep) SOUR CREAM YOGURT (with lactose)

DRIED FRUIT AND SEEDS

Allowed	Allowed in limited quantities	Avoid
BRAZILIAN WALNUTS	ALMONDS	CASHEWS
CHIA SEEDS	ALMOND CREAM	PISTACHIOS
DEHYDRATED BANANA	ALMOND FLOUR	DATES
MACADAMIA NUTS	CRANBERRIES	DRIED FIGS and all other types of dried fruit
MIXED NUTS	COCONUT GRATED, DRIED	GOJI BERRIES
PEANUT BUTTER	HAZELNUTS	
PEANUTS	HAZELNUTS CREAM	
PECAN NUTS	RAISINS	
PINE NUTS	TAHIN (Sesame cream)	
POPPY SEEDS		
PUMPKIN SEEDS		
SUNFLOWER SEEDS		
SESAME		
WALNUTS		

LEGUMES

Allowed	Allowed in limited quantities	Avoid
LENTILS* (canned)	CHICKPEAS (canned)	All others legumes
	PEAS	
	WHITE BEANS (canned)	
	LENTILS (boiled)	

* Only canned legumes **are allowed** - in moderation - because they contain less FODMAPs than dry legumes: Oligo-saccharides and GOS, in fact, are water-soluble, therefore they are dispersed in the preservation liquid. Remember to **rinse** legumes **well** before consuming them.

DRINKS

Allowed	Allowed in limited quantities	Avoid
ALMOND MILK	BLACK TEA	CHAMOMILE
BEER *	COCONUT WATER	DESSERT WINE
COCONUT MILK	FRESH ORANGE JUICE	FENNEL, HERBAL TEA
COFFEE *	LIGHT DANDELION HERBAL TEA	FRUIT JUICES (except raspberry and orange juice)
GIN *		OAT MILK
HEMP MILK		RUM
MILK (Lactose-free)		SOY MILK (from soy beans)
PEPPERMINT HERBAL		
RASPBERRY JUICE		
RICE MILK		
SOY MILK (from soy protein, not from soy beans)		
TEA GREEN		
TEA WHITE		
VODKA *		
WHISKEY *		
WINE *		

* although coffee and alcohol are not high FODMAP, they are nonetheless irritating to the intestine. **Consume them in moderation**

SWEETS AND SWEETENERS

Allowed	Allowed in limited quantities	Avoid
All fruit jams with sweeteners allowed.	MILK CHOCOLATE	HONEY
DARK CHOCOLATE	WHITE CHOCOLATE	AGAVE
COCOA	CAROB FLOUR	FRUCTOSE SYRUP
STEVIA		INULIN
WHITE SUGAR		ISOMALT
BROWN SUGAR		MALTITOL
MAPLE SYRUP		MANNITOL
RICE SYRUP		SORBITOL
GLUCOSE SYRUP		XYLITOL

CONDIMENTS

Allowed	Allowed in limited quantities	Avoid
ALL HERBS	BALSAMIC VINEGAR	TZATZIKI
ALL SPICES	WHITE VINEGAR	HUMMUS
ALL TYPES OF OIL		KETCHUP
APPLE CIDER VINEGAR		
BARBECUE SAUCE		
CANNED TOMATOES		
MAYONNAISE		
MISO		
MUSTARD		
RICE VINEGAR		
SOY SAUCE		
WASABI		
WORCESTERSHIRE SAUCE		

VEGAN ALTERNATIVES

Allowed	Allowed in limited quantities	Avoid
MARGARINE		FALAFEL
TEMPEH		
TOFU		

Phase 5: High-FODMAPs Reintroduction

After you've completed the low-FODMAP diet, it's time to reintroduce high-FODMAPs back into your diet. The goal of this phase is to identify what exactly triggers sensitivity in your gut. However, when reintroducing high-FODMAPS, it is recommended to do so slowly, trying one or two high-FODMAPS at a time.

For instance, you can start out by reintroducing lactose into your diet, which can be as little as one cup of dairy-based milk to see how your body responds. During this phase, you'll be required to continue documenting your meals and describing how it is you feel after each meal in which you reintroduce certain types of food. Be sure to make notes on how these foods make you feel and whether it causes you to have any symptoms. A low-FODMAP app on your smartphone is also a great option for tracking your meals, progress, and symptoms. This phase can take anywhere between six and eight weeks. During this period, you must continue to follow a low-FODMAP diet to identify any potential triggers of symptoms you may have, which can help you during the last phase, which is to personalize your diet and lifestyle, permanently eliminating foods that don't accommodate well with your body.

Since you have four to eight weeks to play with, be sure to test every possible high-FODMAP you can, and don't test too many different ones on a single given day. Even though the low-FODMAP diet is designed to be a temporary diet, the personalization of your own diet in phase six, after reintroducing high-FODMAPs and discovering what you can consume versus what not to, you will be creating a somewhat "forever" diet to support your condition and sustain your future gut health. It doesn't have to be strict, but it will have to exclude the foods that still continue to disrupt your gastrointestinal tract after you've reintroduced it into your diet.

The incredible thing about the low-FODMAP diet is that it is possible for you to have been sensitive to certain high-FODMAPs before you've embarked on the elimination phase that you won't be sensitive to after reintroducing it into your diet. That means that you could possibly tolerate some troublesome foods in a low quantity, which should be maintained in lower quantities in your diet.

Phase 6: Diet and Lifestyle Personalization

After the reintroduction of high-FODMAPs into your diet, you now know what causes or aggravates IBS symptoms in your body. By permanently eliminating the FODMAPs that are bothersome in your diet, and maintaining a low-FODMAP-based diet with high-FODMAPs that are welcomed by your body, you will be able to personalize a diet that suits all your needs. Some high-FODMAP foods that still trigger your symptoms can usually be consumed in very low quantities every other day and shouldn't affect the body negatively.

When personalizing your diet, you can also adjust your entire lifestyle to improve your health, stress management, body composition, and best of all, your condition. Finding a perfect balance of what's good for your body and eliminating that which isn't is a great way to manage IBS effectively, and living the best life you possibly can for as long as you can.

About the Low-FODMAP Diet

Getting started on the low-FODMAP diet, the number one thing to do is be realistic. Often, people quit their diets, fitness routines, and lifestyle changes because they are not seeing results right away. As with any other diet, you can't give this one a week and decide that it's not working, so it's probably not for you. In that same breath, you also can't approach the low-FODMAP diet with half the mentality of doing it but refrain from planning at all.

Some people insist that they can't plan, and they rather prefer to just go with it, as it places too much pressure on them to reach an expectation. However, setting a goal for yourself and planning the steps on how you're going to achieve it is quite necessary for you to successfully complete the diet. This diet is not designed as a weight-loss method and won't promise you any substantial weight loss either, which is usually something that grabs people's attention to start a diet in the first place. On the flip side, this diet can treat a condition that is considered to be quite difficult to manage otherwise, and while living with it is a grave challenge, it's a relief to know that there are proven ways to manage it effectively. Even though the low-FODMAP diet is not a 100% symptom relief diet, it can provide you with more than 50% improvement in symptoms in a matter of weeks, which could be life-changing for people living with IBS.

When you feel like you're struggling with the diet, just remember why you've decided to start it. Lack of motivation shouldn't be a factor here, as the reason for the diet is quite purposeful. Can you lose weight on the low-FODMAP diet? Of course, you can, but the main focus still remains to treat your condition and become as healthy as you possibly can.

Remember to keep in mind that where your focus goes, your energy is bound to flow.

Alternative High-FODMAP Options

AGAVE AND HONEY	MAPLE SYRUP OR LIGHT CORN SYRUP
BREADCRUMBS	PANKO CRUMBS
COUSCOUS	BROWN RICE, WHITE RICE, AND QUINOA
FLOUR (WHEAT)	gluten-free flours containing xanthan gum. avoid gluten-free flours with **ALMONDS, CHICKPEAS, AND OTHER HIGH-FODMAP INGREDIENTS**
KETCHUP	**ORGANIC KETCHUP** with minimal seasonings and no high-fructose ingredients
MILK	LACTOSE-FREE MILK, SUCH AS RICE MILK, ALMOND MILK, HEMP MILK, AND COCONUT MILK
MOLASSES	BROWN RICE SYRUP OR DARK CORN SYRUP
GARLIC AND ONION POWDERS	**ASAFETIDA** OR **INFUSED OILS**, both of which can contain a similar flavor as garlic and onion powder. consider replacing garlic and onions with **CHIVES** and **GREEN PARTS OF ONION SPRINGS** too.

PASTA OR NOODLES	RICE NOODLES, GLUTEN-FREE PASTA WITH CORN OR RICE FLOURS, RISOTTO, OR SOBA NOODLES
WHIPPED CREAMS	COCONUT CREAM

Diet Pitfalls to Avoid

You're possibly restricting yourself

FODMAP restrictions can affect your gut flora negatively, which can be quite dangerous for the proper functioning of your digestive system. To prevent this from happening, you should eat a very large variety of foods. Eating a nutrient-dense diet can help you thrive with or without a gastrointestinal disorder, such as IBS.

You're not actually following a low-FODMAP diet

There's a fine line between what's considered low-FODMAP foods and high-FODMAP foods. It could be that you think you're following the low-FODMAP diet, but you're still eating certain high-FODMAPs. This is usually because there's a possibility of sneaky ingredients added to food items. If you've eaten a lot of processed foods in the past, it can also be quite difficult to identify the difference between low-FODMAP and high-FODMAP ingredients, especially when it comes to only being allowed to eat certain types of flours compared to wheat-based flours. It could also be that you're so used to eating certain types of food, mostly high-FODMAP, that you find it very difficult to eat alternative types of food. If you're used to eating out a lot, it's also best to reduce the number of meals you eat outside of your kitchen to ensure you're only eating low-FODMAP ingredients. Only then will you know whether you're eating only low-FODMAPs.

Non-FODMAP foods that are responsible for your symptoms

It may come as a shock to you, but other than high-FODMAP foods, there are potentially more foods you'll have to avoid to see whether it affects the presence of symptoms related to your condition. To avoid additional triggers in your diet, you can consult your dietician to rule out the following or eliminate it one at a time to see whether it's affecting you.

- Not drinking the proper amount of water, which can cause constipation

- Indulging in too much fat, causing pain, wind, bloating, and diarrhea

- The presence of spicy foods in your diet that can cause heartburn and pain

- Caffeine can cause diarrhea and stomach pain

- Alcohol can cause indigestion, pain, nausea, and diarrhea

- Medications, such as antibiotics, which are recommended for IBS patients for pain relief, can aggravate symptoms and cause side effects, should it not be compatible with a patient's dietary needs

- Gluten and dairy as active ingredients in non-FODMAPs can cause bloating, constipation, pain, and diarrhea

You're following the low-FODMAP diet but are still experiencing symptoms

Your diet is just one element that affects and contributes to your condition. Your lifestyle is the second-biggest contributor and can cause you to continue experiencing symptoms that could otherwise be ruled out if you were living a healthy lifestyle. Focusing on your habits, it's important to take time and reflect on whether there's something you could possibly adjust or do better, such as the times of the day you've designated for your meals, how or whether you take time to manage stress, a lack of exercising, as well as a lack of sleep. Even if your diet is perfect, if you don't have these factors set in place, your gut could be affected negatively. It will also affect how food is digested and absorbed inside your body and cause symptoms, such as bloating, stomach pain, constipation or diarrhea.

When it comes to managing your symptoms, adjusting your habits before you start the low-FODMAP diet is a great way of establishing a foundation for your health that you can add on with the help of the low-FODMAP diet. Improving your quality of sleep can result in the improved functioning of your entire body. Combating stress and finding ways to deal with it more effectively, such as incorporating regular exercise, mediation, or even practicing mindfulness by journaling, are all great ways to relax the body, all of which will support an active metabolism and promote proper digestion.

You're undermining the extent of your condition

The reason why it's so important to have a doctor diagnose you with IBS is that there are many other conditions you could potentially have other than IBS itself. It's also possible that you require regular medical checkups based on the extent of your condition. If you have other conditions in conjunction with IBS, you may have a more difficult time treating your symptoms by just altering your diet. In this case, dieticians may also prescribe a strict diet for you. However, when it comes to IBS alone, the low-FODMAP diet can treat both IBS-D and IBS-C successfully. It is important to raise any possible concerns with your doctor or dietician about your journey on the diet. If you're experiencing persistent symptoms after following the low-FODMAP diet and adjusting your lifestyle, you may need more extensive medical advice and care.

You don't have IBS

That's one thing you should definitely clear up with your doctor before attempting the low-FODMAP diet. Yes, this diet is good for treating various digestive disorders, but there are other disorders that are considered to have even worse effects on the body than IBS, such as SIBO, inflammatory bowel disease, celiac disease, a leaky gut, and endometriosis in women, all of which are conditions your doctor can test you for, should the low-FODMAP diet fail to relieve your symptoms.

Keeping possible diet pitfalls in mind, if you're still experiencing your symptoms to the extent you did before starting the low-FODMAP diet, ask yourself:

1. Do you have realistic expectations?
2. Are you faking the low-FODMAP diet or possibly eating high-FODMAP foods?
3. Is it necessary to consult more than one doctor to diagnose your condition or review the extensity of your condition?
4. Are you demotivated by the diet and giving up?
5. Is your lifestyle affecting your results on the diet, and can you adjust it to improve your symptoms?
6. Are other foods triggering your symptoms?
7. Do you really have IBS?
8. Are other conditions preventing you from treating IBS symptoms?

FAQ

How long does phase one to phase six of the diet last?

Phase one, two, and three are entirely up to you and based on when you'd like to start. Taking a week or two to consult your doctor, a dietician, educate yourself, plan your meals, buy the ingredients you need for the week, and perhaps even get crafty with recipes will be beneficial and set the tone for your journey. By putting in the effort to plan and prep meals, you are more likely to remain disciplined throughout the process.

Phase four typically lasts between two to six weeks, which depends on how soon you see results after eliminating high-FODMAPs from your diet. If your symptoms improve consistently, you've managed to recognize different stressors and lifestyle factors that affect your digestion negatively and have reached a point of being comfortable to eat a low-FODMAP diet without constraint, you can move on to the next phase. However, don't rush the elimination phase. Take the time you need to relieve your gut symptoms before you reintroduce possible trigger foods back into your diet.

Phase five is the high-FODMAP reintroduction phase, which can last anywhere between six to eight weeks so that you have time to reintroduce different high-FODMAPs back into your diet one at a time, as well as the effects they have on your condition and its symptoms. Considering how it makes you feel will also provide you with a good indication of whether your body is welcoming to it.

Phase six is all about personalizing your diet after you've established which food you can eat and those that you can't. By this point, you should be able to identify what's good for your body and make decisions accordingly, both food-based and lifestyle-based to nurture and support the healthiest version of yourself possible.

How do I know whether it's the right time to

switch from the elimination phase to the reintroduction of the high-FODMAPs phase?

The right time to switch from phase four to phase five is when your symptoms have been relieved. If your symptoms are immediately relieved, consider giving the elimination phase more time to ensure your symptoms are reduced as much as possible. The elimination phase should be completed in two to six weeks, depending on how fast it works for you. The longer you take to complete it, the better. Only then can you switch to the reintroduction of the high-FODMAPs phase. Before you switch to phase five, also be sure to note how you're feeling overall and whether you feel ready to start reintroducing high-FODMAP foods back into your diet.

How do I stay motivated on the low-FODMAP diet?

While staying on track with any diet is a challenge, you can motivate yourself by setting micro-goals, such as getting through the first seven days of the elimination phase before considering continuing with another week or few weeks. By setting micro-goals instead of telling yourself that you have to follow the elimination phase for six weeks, you'll have a better chance of sticking to your diet, which will also allow you to reap more benefits from the diet, ultimately inspiring you to continue with the diet.

How do I track my progress?

Keeping a journal, apart from a food journal, will help you document how you feel about not only the foods you eat but also about how you feel in general. Consider whether you feel stressed or review your emotions daily. Write it down and find ways to deal with it accordingly. Once you implement those changes, you can also reflect on whether you're feeling better. This can be done in every aspect of your life, even with your eating habits, meal sizes, and sleeping patterns, and can lead to you achieving your ultimate state of wellness in mind, body, and spirit.

Will my symptoms reappear after I've finished the high-FODMAP reintroduction phase?

Not necessarily. The point of the low-FODMAP diet's elimination phase is to remove possible gut-triggering foods from your diet, all of which can potentially worsen IBS symptoms. The phase that follows, the reintroduction phase, is designed to allow you to test whether certain foods can be reintroduced into your diet or not. Those that you reintroduce and still cause a negative reaction in your body in the form of symptoms should be avoided completely. Only then will your symptoms be relieved after you've completed the low-FODMAP diet.

What should I do if the low-FODMAP diet doesn't work?

You should consult your doctor or dietician to explore other possible reasons why you still have symptoms. It could be that you suffer from other underlying conditions, such as endometriosis, inflammatory bowel disease, SIBO, celiac disease, or a leaky gut.

Can the low-FODMAP diet treat other gastrointestinal disorders?

When you are diagnosed with other gastrointestinal disorders or digestive issues, it's always better to consult with your doctor or dietician about a diet specifically designed to treat your disorder. This is especially important in people with gut-related issues, as the last thing you want to do is aggravate your gut symptoms. However, the low-FODMAP diet is a well-structured diet that is focused on bringing balance to the gut, ensuring that there are no possible foods included in the diet that could trigger potential gastrointestinal symptoms, such as bloating, gas, stomach pain, constipation, or diarrhea.

Can boosting the vagal tone of the vagus nerve really improve my health?

Stimulating the vagus nerve by improving vagal tone can significantly support the healthy functioning of many processes and functions in your body ranging from your brain and branching out to the rest of your body. It can reduce stress in the body, which can promote the health of your organs, digestive system, respiratory system, neurons, nerves, muscles, tendons, and joints. It can also combat gastrointestinal disorders by ensuring the intestines and colon aren't stressed or become spastic, promoting regular bowels and digestive health every day.

I am going to have to stay on this diet forever?

A long-term restriction is definitely not the goal. The main goal of this diet is to reintroduce as many foods back into your diet as possible. The way foods are reintroduced and permanently removed will have to be decided during the process.

Why are there restrictions on onion and garlic but the infused oils are safe to use?

FODMAPs are soluble in water, but they are not in fat. When an onion is placed into a stock or broth, it will leave the FODMAPs behind in the mixture when removed. In an oil-based mixture, the flavor is left behind but the FODMAPS do not linger.

Can I have a cheat day?

This is a big no-no when it comes to this diet. When removing the high-FODMAPS, the goal is to let the body expel the high-FODMAPS so there is a clean slate to start the reintroduction process. Having even a small amount of high-FODMAPs will set you back, and the process will need to be started from scratch.

Am I going to be able to eat the foods I love again?

The main goal is to get back to the point where only the minimum food items are cut out of your diet. However, there is a large number of people who are content to avoid certain high-FODMAPs almost completely.

When will I notice improvements?

It depends on the individual. Some notice changes in 48 hours, while it can take weeks for others to notice even the smallest improvement.

Meal Plan

When looking at making a healthy change in eating habits, a meal plan can be the difference between success and failure. This section is aimed at helping kick-start the low-FODMAP diet. While the meal plan is used as an example, it is also intended to teach how this diet can be implemented. The plan is to put a structure in place to create a habit of healthy living. The menu can be changed easily by changing meals every week. An example of this is switching a smoothie for breakfast on day 1 in the first cycle with a basil omelet on day 1 in the second cycle.

At the beginning of a diet, it can be extremely easy to cook food that is convenient, such as pre-cooked meals or to go to a restaurant or get fast food. These convenient meal sources can derail a diet before it has a chance to show any benefits.

Broadly speaking, a meal plan lays out what is for dinner a week or even 7 days before it is time to cook. There are three main components involved in meal planning: selecting meals and their recipes, shopping for ingredients, and preparing the ingredients. These components work in conjunction to benefit your health as well as your finances. Laying out a meal plan allows for healthy eating to be done on a budget; this creates a way to ensure that when life happens, the diet is not the first thing to get thrown out the door. However, before jumping into planning, it is important to understand the diet you are trying out and how to create a functional meal plan that suits your life.

The first thing to do is read up on the diet you are starting, which, in this context, will be the low-FODMAP diet. This knowledge creates the platform for removing high-FODMAP ingredients and reintroducing them in a controlled way.

After gaining a better knowledge of the diet, it is time to start constructing the first meal plan. To begin, it is a good idea to print out a sheet of paper that lays out the days of the week and has space to write down the meals that need to be planned; include meals that are not being eaten at home. With the week's plan laid out, the real work can begin.

It is time to decide on what will be eaten, including recipes. If you are planning for a family, it is fun to choose meals together to allow everyone to have a meal that they specifically want to eat. At first, the easiest thing to do may be to mainly plan dinners, marking down the difficulty of the recipes. Breakfasts and lunches can be partially planned until you have more confidence; however, this is only if you are easing into the diet. If you are eliminating all FODMAPS from the get-go, thoroughly planning out breakfasts and lunches is a good idea.

Once meals have been planned, the shopping list needs to be written. The easiest way to do this is to go through each meal and write down what ingredients are needed. These lists are best done once a week so that the ingredients you are using are fresh. Having fresh ingredients is ideal as this increases the nutrients you get with each meal. While there are many ingredients, like fruits and vegetables, that should be bought weekly, there are a few ingredients that can be stocked to cut costs. Some ingredients that can be stocked are sugar, flour, oils, and frozen produce.

Meal planning does not just help with eating healthy; the planning that is involved creates other benefits. Having a menu planned will lower the amount of stress in day-to-day life. You also save time because you already know what to buy and what needs to be cooked. To help save more time, it can be useful to prepare parts of the meals at the beginning of the week. This can be done by preparing and portioning out the meat and vegetables.

For many people, meals become boring because they end up eating the same dishes. When creating a meal plan, there is a small chance of dishes being overly repeated. By adding new dishes into your diet, there is an improvement in digestion as the different nutrients are introduced into the body. With each meal set out, it is also easier to prevent food waste. By planning out portions, the ingredients are used with minimum waste, which saves money spent on more ingredients.

A tip to save money and create less waste is to plan backward. At the end of a week or month, it is a good idea to look at what ingredients you still have in your fridge and freezer. Using these ingredients, you can create a menu that first uses the ingredients you still have before you do a shopping trip for the week.

The biggest tip for meal planning is to develop a routine. Developing a routine will make it easier to eat healthily and improve your overall lifestyle.

Meal Plan

This menu serves as a visual aid of what meals will be eaten when. It must be noted that recipes can be swapped with different meals to create a more balanced menu. This first menu lays out the meals in a simple but not strict manner. This allows for the development of the diet as time goes by. As menus, the two examples do not look at the strict serving information; they are guidelines to work from. The first menu gives not only the meals but also the way to plan a shopping list.

Menu 1

DAY	1	2	3	4	5	6	7
Breakfast	Basic Smoothie Berry pag.112	Tomato omelet pag. 136	Quinoa porridge pag. 130	Green smoothie pag. 124	Egg wrap pag.118	Peanut butter bowl pag.126	Fluffy pancakes pag. 122
Lunch	Chicken wrap pag. 142	Corn Salad pag. 146	Rice paper spring rolls pag. 158	Hawaiian toasted Sandwich pag. 148	Carrot & walnut salad pag. 140	Thai noodle soup pag. 160	Tropical smoothie pag. 164
Dinner	Coconut crusted fish pag. 176	Baked chicken alfredo pag. 168	Bolognese pag. 170	Tofu Skewers pag. 188	Burgers pag. 172	Lamb stew pag. 182	Cheesy chicken pag. 174
Snack	Vegetable chips pag. 204		Salted caramel pumpkin seed pag. 198				Summer popsicles pag. 202
Drinks	8 cups Water	8 cups Water	8 cups Water	8 cups Water	8 cups Water	8 cups Water	8 cups Water

Scan QR code to download this list

Shopping List for Menu 1

Vegetables
- 2 bunches baby spinach
- 1 bunch kale
- 12 tomatoes
- 25 cherry tomatoes
- 6 cucumbers (3 small, 3 large)
- 1 red capsicum
- 2 heads of lettuce
- 22 carrots
- 1 parsnip
- 5 potatoes
- 1 red cabbage
- 5 spring onions
- ⅓ lb green beans
- 1 head of broccoli

Fruits
- 3 bananas
- 16 oz strawberries
- 1 pineapple
- 1 can of pineapple
- 5 limes
- 6 lemons
- 6 oranges
- 16 oz mixed berries
- ¼ cup dried, shredded coconut
- 4 oz olives

Protein
- 8 eggs
- 1 lb lamb, deboned
- 1 lb white fish
- 12 chicken breast fillets
- 2 lbs lean ground beef
- 6 ham slices

Dairy
- 1 pt Greek yogurt
- 2 pts almond milk
- 2 pts oat milk
- 2 cans coconut milk
- 1 bottle mayonnaise
- 1 block butter
- 1 block cheddar
- 1 block Parmesan
- 10 slices mozzarella

Grains
- ⅓ cup flaxseed
- 2 lbs gluten-free flour
- 1 packet gluten-free pasta
- ½ lb pumpkin seeds
- ½ lb walnuts
- ½ lb pecans
- ½ lb chestnuts
- ½ lb quinoa, uncooked
- 1 packet rice noodles
- 4 gluten-free wraps
- 1 loaf gluten-free bread
- ½ dozen gluten-free buns
- 12 rice paper wrappers

Condiments
- 1 jar smooth peanut butter
- 1 jar maple syrup
- 1 can miso paste
- 1 bottle soy sauce
- 2 cans tomato purée
- 1 can tomato paste

Sweeteners
- ¾ cup vanilla extract
- 1 lb white sugar
- 1 lb brown sugar

Herbs & spices
- 2 mild green chilis
- 1 bunch mint
- ¾ cup ginger, ground and crushed
- ¾ cup basil, fried
- 1 bunch fresh basil
- 8 lime leaves
- ¾ cup cinnamon, ground
- ¾ cup nutmeg, ground
- ¾ cup cumin
- 2 bunches cilantro
- 4 tbsp chili flakes
- 1 bunch sage
- ¾ cup oregano, dried

Liquids
- ½ cup vegetable stock, no garlic or onion

Oils
- 1 bottle olive oil
- 1 bottle sunflower oil
- 1 bottle garlic-infused oil
- 1 bottle Worcestershire sauce

Dry baking ingredients
- 1 ½ lbs powdered sugar

Menu 2

DAY	1	2	3	4	5	6	7
Breakfast	Scrambled Tofu **pag. 132**	2 energy bars **pag.120**	Smoothie bowl **pag. 134**	Crepes **pag.116**	Basil omelet **pag. 114**	Kale ginger pineapple smoothie **pag. 125**	Quinoa muffin **pag. 128**
Lunch	Quiche in ham cups **pag.156**	Corn on the cob **pag.144**	Pesto sandwich **pag.152**	Tomato & green bean salad **pag.162**	Smoothie basic coconut **pag.112**	Frittata **pag. 150**	Pineapple & yogurt rice cakes **pag. 154**
Dinner	Zucchini fritters **pag. 192**	Pork tacos **pag.186**	Fresh vegetables & beetroot dip **pag. 178**	Fried rice **pag.180**	Frittata **pag. 150**	Tuna, bacon quinoa bowl **pag. 190**	Pesto noodles **pag.184**
Snack			chia pudding **pag. 196**				strawberry ice cream **pag. 200**
Drinks	8 cups Water	8 cups Water	8 cups Water	8 cups Water	8 cups Water	8 cups Water	8 cups Water

Scan QR code to download this list

Shopping List for Menu 2

Vegetables
- 6 tomatoes
- 2 spring onions
- 1 head of lettuce
- 1 bunch kale
- 12 carrots
- 2 cucumbers (1 small, 1 large)
- 2 zucchinis
- ½ lb green beans
- 20 cherry tomatoes
- 2 red bell peppers
- ½ lb sweet potatoes
- ¼ lb leeks
- 6 ears of corn
- 1 head of broccoli

Fruits
- 14 bananas
- 7 oz strawberries
- 4 oz mixed berries
- 4 oz cranberries
- 3 limes
- 1 orange
- 1 can of pineapple
- 1 lemon

Protein
- 2 dozen eggs
- ½ lb pork loin
- 2 chicken breast fillets
- 6 ham slices
- ½ lb bacon
- 1 can shredded tuna in brine
- 5 oz firm tofu

Dairy
- 1 pt Greek yogurt
- ¾ pt coconut yogurt
- 1 can coconut milk
- ½ cup dark chocolate
- ½ cup mozzarella cheese
- 1 pt lactose-free milk

Grains
- ½ lb gluten-free oat flour
- 1 loaf gluten-free bread
- ½ lb rice flour
- 6 corn tortillas
- Rice cakes
- ¾ lb uncooked rice
- 1 packet rice noodles
- 1 cup quinoa flakes
- 1 lb puffed rice
- ¾ cup pumpkin seeds

Condiments
- 1 jar Dijon mustard
- ⅔ cup red wine vinegar
- 6 oz pesto, no garlic or onion

Sweeteners
None

Herbs & spices
- ¾ cup chives
- 1 cup chia seeds
- ¾ cup smoked paprika
- 1 jalapeño
- ¾ cup turmeric, ground

Liquids
None

Oils
- 1 bottle sesame oil
- 1 bottle rice vinegar

Dry baking ingredients
None

Measurement Conversions

Volume equivalents (Liquid)

US standard	US Ounces	Metric (approximate)
2 tablespoons	1 fl. Oz.	30 mL
¼ cup	2 fl. Oz.	60 mL
½ cup	4 fl. Oz.	120 mL
1 cup	8 fl. Oz.	240 mL
1½ cup	12 fl. Oz.	355 mL
2 cups or 1 pint	16 fl. Oz.	475 mL
4 cups or 1 quart	32 fl. Oz.	1 L
1 gallon	128 fl. Oz.	4 L

Volume equivalents (Dry)

US standard	Metric (approximate)
⅛ teaspoon	0.5 mL
¼ teaspoon	1 mL
½ teaspoon	2 mL
¾ teaspoon	4 mL
1 teaspoon	5 mL
1 tablespoon	15 mL
¼ cup	59 mL
⅓ cup	79 mL
½ cup	118 mL
⅔ cup	156 mL
¾ cup	177 mL
1 cup	235 mL
2 cups or 1 pint	475 mL
3 cups	700 mL
4 cups or 1 quart	1 L

Oven Temperatures

Fahrenheit	Celsius (approximate)
250° F	120° C
300° F	150° C
325° F	165° C
350° F	180° C
375° F	190° C
400° F	200° C
425° F	220° C
450° F	230° C

Weight Equivalents

US Standard	Metric (approximate)
½ ounce	15 g
1 ounce	30 g
2 ounces	60 g
4 ounces	115 g
8 ounces	225 g
12 ounces	340 g
16 ounces or 1 pound	455 g

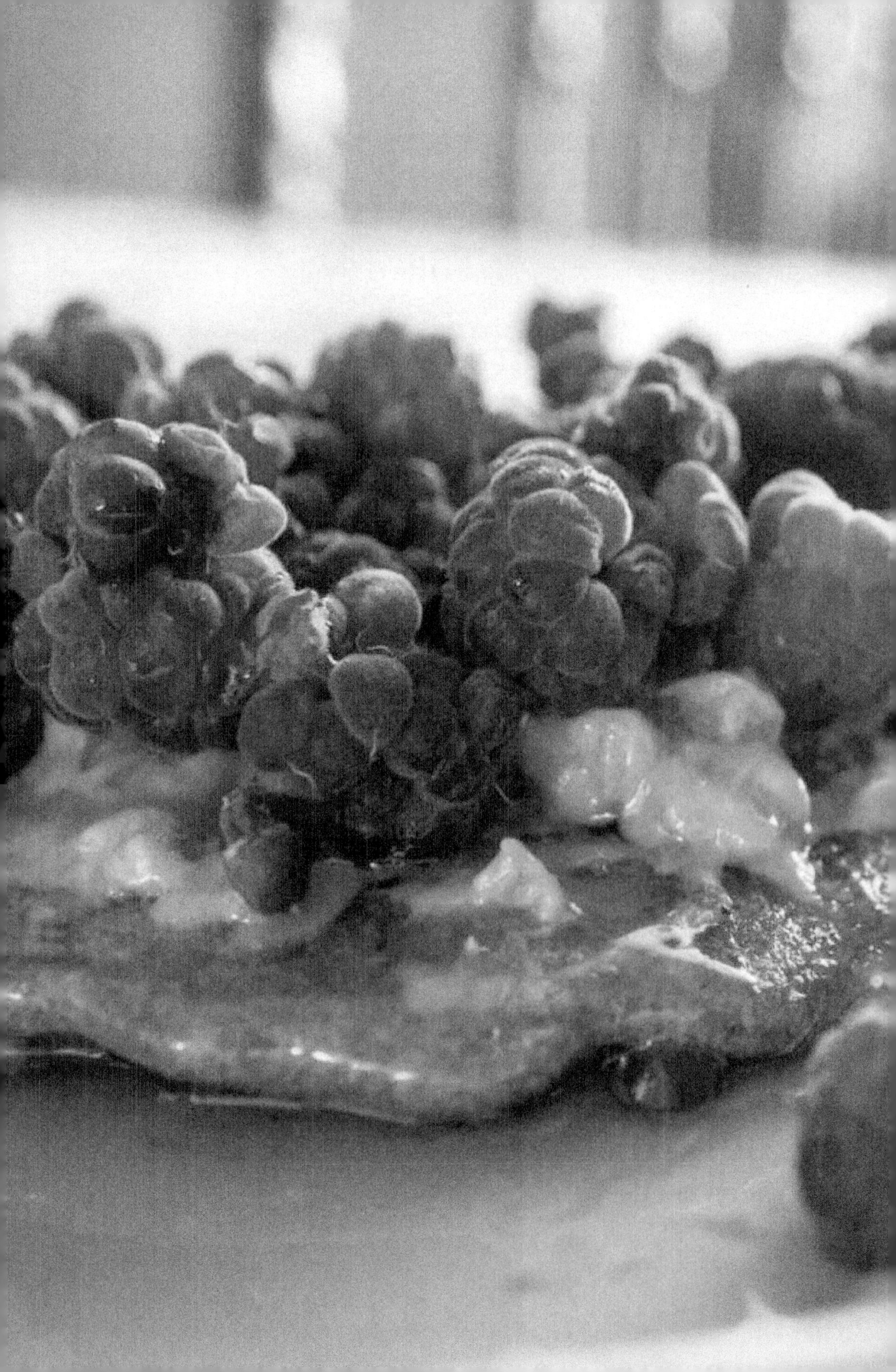

BREAKFAST

Basic Smoothie Berry 112

Basil omelet 114

Crepes and Berries 116

Egg wrap 118

energy bars 120

Fluffy pancakes 122

Green smoothie 124

Kale ginger pineapple smoothie 125

Peanut butter bowl 126

Quinoa muffin 128

Quinoa porridge 130

Scrambled Tofu 132

Smoothie bowl 134

Tomato omelet 136

Basic Smoothie Base

Difficulty: Easy

Preparation time: 2 minutes

Cook time: 3 minutes

Servings: 1

Ingredients

Base *

- 1 banana, sliced and frozen
- ¾ cup Greek yogurt
- 2 tbsp almond milk
- ¼ tsp vanilla extract
- ¼ cup ice, optional

Flavoring variations

Choconut *

- 1 tbsp peanut butter
- 1 tbsp cocoa powder
- Pinch of salt

Berry *

- ½ cup strawberries, can be replaced with any other approved berry or a mixture
- 5 mint leaves
- Pinch of salt

Tropical *

- 1 cup papaya, peeled and diced
- 1 tbsp lime juice
- Pinch of salt

Method

1. In a blender, add the base ingredients and one of the flavor combinations.

2. If ice is added, drink immediately or cover and put in the fridge.

Cal 334 — Base *

Nutrition per serving (g)

Fat	Saturates	Carbs	Sugars	Fiber	Protein	Salt
17	10	36	23	3	9	0.5

Cal 430 — Base + Choconut *

Nutrition per serving (g)

Fat	Saturates	Carbs	Sugars	Fiber	Protein	Salt
26	13	42	24	6	14	0.3

Cal 353 — Base + Berry *

Nutrition per serving (g)

Fat	Saturates	Carbs	Sugars	Fiber	Protein	Salt
18	10	43	26	5	10	0.3

Cal 383 — Base + Tropical *

Nutrition per serving (g)

Fat	Saturates	Carbs	Sugars	Fiber	Protein	Salt
18	11	51	31	6	10	0.2

Basil Omelet with Smashed Tomato

Cal 175.5
VEGETARIAN

Difficulty: Easy
Preparation time: 5 minutes
Cook time: 10 minutes
Servings: 2

Nutrition per serving (g)

Fat	Saturates	Carbs	Sugars	Fiber	Protein	Salt
10.5	48	6	4	1.5	14.5	0.2

Ingredients

- 2 tomatoes, halved
- 3 eggs
- 1 tbsp chives, chopped
- ¼ cup shredded mozzarella cheese (or other FODMAP-approved cheese)
- 1-2 basil leaves, chopped finely
- Pepper

Method

1. Break the eggs into a bowl and add a splash of water. Whisk the mixture with a fork and add the chives and a pinch of pepper. Set aside.

2. Place the halved tomatoes on tinfoil in a hot skillet on the stove or onto a hot grill on low to medium heat. Turn occasionally until they are starting to char, then remove them and place them on plates. Squish slightly so that the juices are released.

3. Take the egg mixture and whisk it slightly before pouring it into a hot pan on medium heat. Leave the mixture for a few seconds before gently stirring the uncooked egg until it is cooked but still slightly loose.

4. Place the cheese and a basil leaf on one half of the egg and then gently fold the omelet in half. Let it cook for another minute. Once it is cooked, cut the omelet in half and serve with the tomato.

Crepes and Berries

Cal 277 **VEGETARIAN**	**Difficulty:** Easy **Preparation time:** 18 minutes **Cook time:** 8 minutes **Servings:** 4							
Nutrition per serving (g)								
Fat	Saturates	Carbs	Sugars	Fiber	Protein	Salt		
10.5	4.5	25	6	3.5	8	0.2		

Ingredients

Crepes

- ½ cup oat flour
- 1 tsp brown sugar
- 1 tsp white sugar
- 2 eggs
- 1 ½ tbsp melted butter
- 1 tsp vanilla extract

Filling

- ½ cup berry mix
- Pinch of brown sugar
- Pinch of cinnamon
- 2 tbsp Greek yogurt

Method

1. In a blender, place the crepe ingredients and blend for two minutes. Set aside to rest for 15 minutes.

2. Mix the brown sugar and cinnamon with the berries.

3. After the crepe mix has rested, place a non-stick pan, greased with oil, over medium heat. Add ¼ cup of the crepe batter to the pan. Gently move the pan to cover the bottom of the pan with a thin layer of batter. Cook for a minute and gently flip.

4. Once the crepes are cooked, place them on a plate and top with a small amount of yogurt, fold, and place the berries on top.

Egg Wraps

Cal 414 VEGETARIAN	**Difficulty:** Easy **Preparation time:** 5 minutes **Cook time:** 5 minutes **Servings:** 4

Nutrition per serving (g)

Fat	Saturates	Carbs	Sugars	Fiber	Protein	Salt
33	8	2	2	0	25	0.2

Ingredients

- Oil to grease the pan
  (from the approved food list: avocado, olive, or sunflower)
- 4-8 eggs
- Pinch of salt
- Pepper

Method

1 Grease a non-stick pan with oil then place over medium heat to warm.

2 Whisk the egg in a bowl and pour it into the pan, ensuring it is spread evenly. Add in salt and pepper to taste.

3 Cook for 30-60 seconds on each side; gently flip when the edges on the first side are cooked.

4 Place on a plate to cool and repeat with the remainder of the eggs.

Tip

When using a small or medium pan (6-8 inches), cook one egg at a time. If using a large pan (10-12 inches), cook 2 eggs at a time.

Energy Bars

Cal 121 VEGETARIAN	Difficulty: Easy Preparation time: 10 minutes Cook time: - Servings: 14 (1 slice per serving)

Nutrition per serving (g)

Fat	Saturates	Carbs	Sugars	Fiber	Protein	Salt
6.4	1	14.4	8.8	1.2	3	0

Ingredients

- ⅓ cup sunflower seed butter or peanut butter
- 6 tbsp maple syrup
- 1 ½ cups puffed rice
- ½ cup pumpkin seeds, roughly chopped
- 4 tbsp dried cranberries, chopped roughly
- ½ tsp ginger, ground
- ½ tsp cinnamon, ground
- 1 tbsp dark chocolate, chopped roughly

Method

1 Line a square baking pan with parchment paper.

2 Melt the butter and the syrup over medium heat. Once melted, remove from the heat and stir in the pumpkin seeds, puffed rice, dried cranberries, ginger, and cinnamon. Coat the ingredients evenly.

3 Spread the mixture across the pan evenly, then place another piece of parchment paper over the mixture and apply pressure evenly to compress.

4 Melt the dark chocolate, then drizzle over the mixture. Refrigerate for 2 hours before cutting.

Fluffy Pancakes

Cal 116 VEGETARIAN

Difficulty: Easy
Preparation time: 10 minutes
Cook time: 15 minutes
Servings: 16 (4 per serving)

Nutrition per serving (g)

Fat	Saturates	Carbs	Sugars	Fiber	Protein	Salt
3.8	2	18.7	9.4	0.2	1.4	0.1

Ingredients

Batter

- 1 ¼ cups gluten-free flour
- 3 tsp baking powder
- 2 tbsp white sugar
- ¾ cup lactose-free or coconut milk
- 1 egg
- ¾ tsp vanilla extract
- 2 tsp butter

Serve

- ½ cup regular fat cream, whipped
- 8 tbsp strawberry jam

Method

1. In a bowl, whisk the dry ingredients and create a well in the middle. Add the milk, egg, and vanilla extract. Mix together until there are almost no lumps.

2. Test the batter. This is done by lifting the whisk out of the bowl. The batter should drizzle thickly back into the bowl; if it is too thick, add a tablespoon of milk.

3. Over medium heat, melt the butter in a non-stick pan. Wipe the pan with a paper towel to remove excess butter.

4. Place 2 tablespoons of batter per pancake into the pan. When bubbles appear on the top of the pancakes, flip them carefully and cook the other side until golden. Serve hot.

Green Smoothie

Cal 121 VEGAN	Difficulty: Easy Preparation time: 3 minutes Cook time: 3 minutes Servings: 1

Nutrition per serving (g)

Fat	Saturates	Carbs	Sugars	Fiber	Protein	Salt
3	0	22	12	6	4	0.2

Ingredients

- ½ cup spinach
- ½ cup kale
- 1 orange, peeled
- 1 tbsp flaxseed
- 1 tbsp ginger, juice or ground
- 1 cup water
  (add more or less depending on the desired consistency)

Combine the ingredients in a blender, then blend to the desired consistency.

Kale, Ginger, and Pineapple Smoothie

Cal 215 VEGAN	Difficulty: Easy Preparation time: 5 minutes Cook time: 2 minutes Servings: 1

Nutrition per serving (g)

Fat	Saturates	Carbs	Sugars	Fiber	Protein	Salt
4	1	37	19	7	10	0.1

Ingredients

- 1 cup FODMAP-approved milk (lactose-free or coconut)
- ½ peeled orange
- ¾ cup pineapple, fresh or frozen
- 1 cup raw kale
- Pinch of ground ginger
- 1 cup ice

Combine the ingredients in a blender, then blend to the desired consistency.

Peanut Butter Bowl

Cal 519
VEGETARIAN

Difficulty: Easy
Preparation time: 3 minutes
Cook time: 5 minutes
Servings: 2

Nutrition per serving (g)

Fat	Saturates	Carbs	Sugars	Fiber	Protein	Salt
35	13.5	5.5	25	5.5	15.5	0.2

Ingredients

- 2 bananas, chopped and frozen
- 1 ½ cups Greek yogurt
- 2 tbsp peanut butter
- ¼ cup chopped nuts

Method

1 In a blender, mix the bananas, yogurt, and peanut butter.

2 When the mixture is a smooth consistency, pour it into a bowl and top with chopped nuts.

Simple!

Quinoa Muffins

Cal 175
VEGETARIAN

Difficulty: Easy
Preparation time: 10 minutes
Cook time: 20 minutes
Servings: 24 muffins (1 per serving)

Nutrition per serving (g)

Fat	Saturates	Carbs	Sugars	Fiber	Protein	Salt
10.5	4	6	4	1.5	14	0.5

Ingredients

- 1 ½ cups quinoa flour
- 1 cup quinoa flakes
- ⅓ cup walnuts, chopped
- 1 tbsp cinnamon
- 4 tsp baking powder
- 2 tsp baking soda
- Pinch of salt
- 4 eggs
- 4 bananas, mashed
- ½ cup almond milk
- ¼ cup maple syrup

Method

1 Preheat the oven to 375°F.

2 Mix the dry ingredients in one bowl. In a separate bowl, combine the wet ingredients. Combine the ingredients until mixed fully.

3 Spoon into greased muffin pans and bake for 20 minutes. Check if the center is dry by poking the center of a muffin with a skewer. If it comes out clean, they are ready.

Quinoa porridge

Cal 292 VEGAN

Difficulty: Easy
Preparation time: 2 minutes
Cook time: 25 minutes
Servings: 2

Nutrition per serving (g)

Fat	Saturates	Carbs	Sugars	Fiber	Protein	Salt
8	1.5	50.5	17	4.5	7.5	0.2

Ingredients

- ½ cup quinoa
- 1 tsp oil (FODMAP-approved)
- 1 cup water
- ¾ cup milk (FODMAP-approved)
- ¼ tsp cinnamon
- 2 tbsp maple syrup
- 1 cup berries (FODMAP-approved)

Method

1. Rinse the quinoa under cold water for two minutes using a fine sieve and then transfer it to a medium saucepan with oil. Toast the quinoa until the water has evaporated.

2. Add water to the saucepan and bring to a boil. Once the water starts boiling, turn the heat down to the lowest setting and cover with a lid. Cook for 12-15 minutes until the quinoa is fluffy. Drain the excess water and place the quinoa back into the saucepan.

3. Mix the cinnamon, milk, and syrup into the quinoa. If the milk evaporates, add a small amount as needed. Let the mix simmer for 5 minutes or until the mixture is warmed through.

4. Serve the mixture in a bowl with berries on top.

Scrambled Tofu

Cal 82 VEGAN	**Difficulty:** Easy **Preparation time:** 5 minutes **Cook time:** 5 minutes **Servings:** 1

Nutrition per serving (g)

Fat	Saturates	Carbs	Sugars	Fiber	Protein	Salt
5	0.5	4	2	0.5	5	0.2

Ingredients

- ½ cup medium-firm tofu
- ¼ cup water
- 1 tbsp soy sauce
- ¼ tsp turmeric, ground
- ½ cup grated carrot and zucchini
- Oil for greasing the pan
- 1 slice FODMAP-approved bread

Method

1. In a bowl, thoroughly mix together the water, soy sauce, and turmeric. Once mixed, add the vegetables and crumble the tofu into the bowl.

2. Place an oil-greased pan onto medium heat and place the mixture in it. Fry the mixture for 5 minutes or until it is golden brown.

3. Serve with a slice of FODMAP-approved toast.

Smoothie Bowl

Cal 324
VEGAN

Difficulty: Easy
Preparation time: 5 minutes
Cook time: 5 minutes
Servings: 2

Nutrition per serving (g)

Fat	Saturates	Carbs	Sugars	Fiber	Protein	Salt
17	10	36	23	3	9	0.5

Ingredients

- 1 cup coconut yogurt
- ½ cup coconut milk, canned or fresh
- 4 bananas, cut into slices and frozen
- 2 cups frozen mixed berries
- 2 tsp lemon juice
- ½ cup mixed nuts, chopped
- 2 mint leaves, torn

Method

1 In a blender, mix yogurt, milk, bananas, frozen berries, and lemon juice.

2 Pour the mix into bowls and top with nuts and mint.

Tomato Omelet

Cal 311.5

VEGETARIAN

Difficulty: Easy
Preparation time: 25 minutes
Cook time: 5 minutes
Servings: 2

Nutrition per serving (g)

Fat	Saturates	Carbs	Sugars	Fiber	Protein	Salt
24	5	10.5	7	3	15	0.2

Ingredients

- 4 fresh tomatoes
- 4 eggs
- ¼ cup water
- ½ tsp chopped basil
- Pinch of salt
- Pinch of pepper
- 2 tbsp olive oil (or other approved oil)

Method

1 Place a pot of water on the stove and bring to a boil. Mark each tomato with an 'x' in the skin and place them in the water. Leave the tomatoes in the water for 30 seconds before removing them with a draining spoon and placing them into cold water.

2 Peel the skin off the tomatoes and cut them in half. Remove the core and seeds and slice into strips. Set them aside.

3 Break the eggs into a bowl and whisk together while adding the basil, salt, and pepper. Stop whisking when the mixture is frothy. Place the mixture into a hot pan that has been greased with oil.

4 Gently stir the mixture while cooking over medium heat. When the mixture starts to get firm, spread the tomato over it. Do not continue stirring the mixture. When the tomatoes are warmed through, remove from the pan and enjoy.

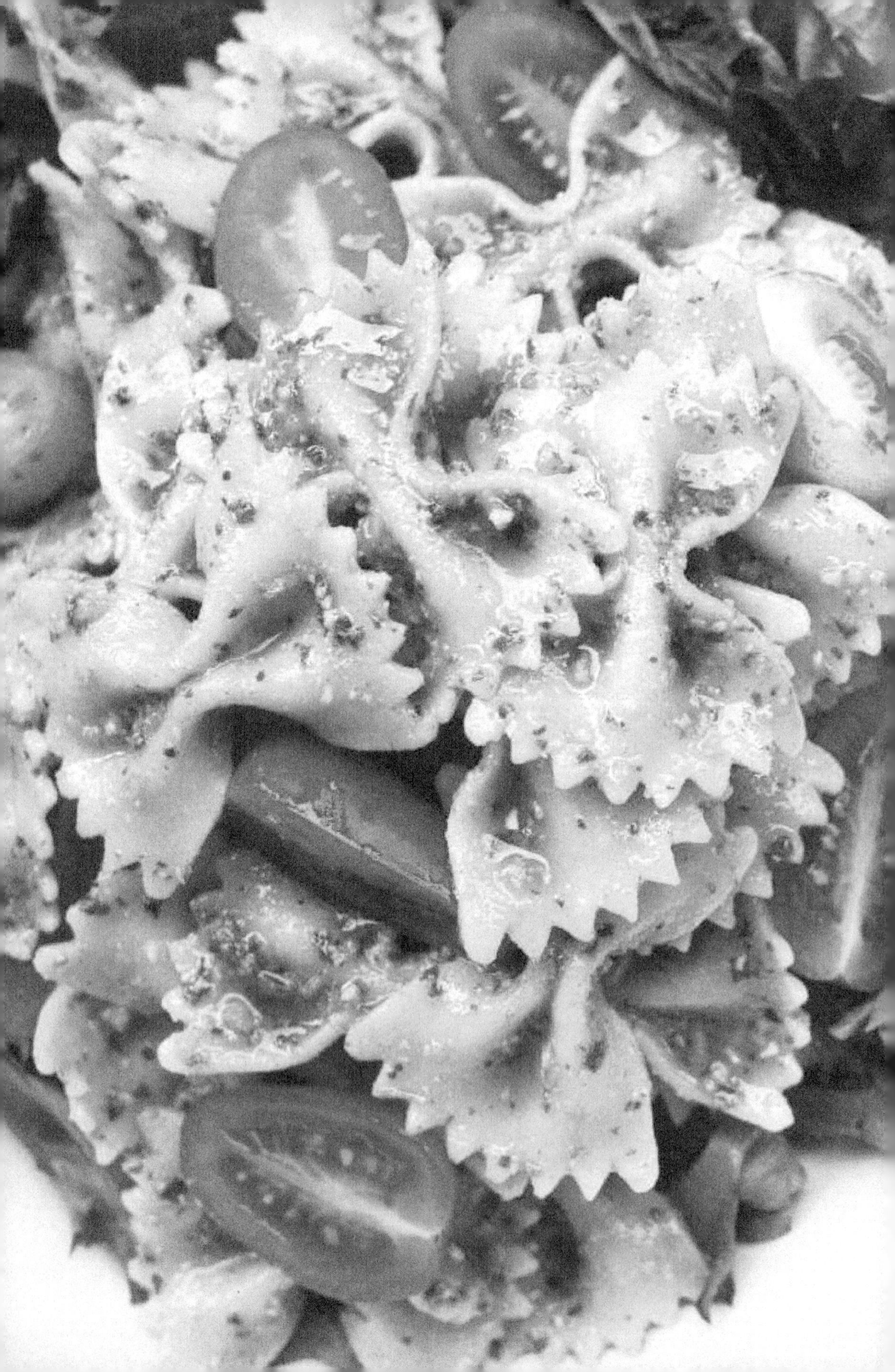

LUNCH

Carrot & walnut salad 140

Chicken wrap 142

Corn on the Cob Corn Salad 144

Frittata 150

Hawaiian toasted Sandwich 148

Pesto Toasted Sandwich 152

Pineapple, Yogurt on Rice Cakes 154

Quiche in Ham Cups 156

Spring Rolls with Satay Sauce 158

Thai Pumpkin Noodle Soup 160

Tomato and Green Bean Salad 162

Tropical smoothie 164

Carrot & Walnut Salad

Cal 277
VEGAN

Difficulty: Easy
Preparation time: 5 minutes
Cook time: 5 minutes
Servings: 4

Nutrition per serving (g)

Fat	Saturates	Carbs	Sugars	Fiber	Protein	Salt
2.4	0.2	7.5	5	2.9	1.7	0.2

Ingredients

- ½ cup lettuce
- 3 carrots, peeled
- ¼ cup walnuts, chopped
- ¼ cup orange juice
- Pinch of salt

Method

1 Wash the lettuce and carrots, and then shred the lettuce into a bowl. Shave the carrots into strips and mix with the lettuce.

2 Place a greased pan over medium heat. Add the walnuts and fry quickly (2 minutes), stirring often to prevent the walnuts from burning. Remove the walnuts from the pan and place onto a paper towel. Sprinkle with salt.

3 Mix the lettuce and carrots in a bowl. Add the orange juice and the walnuts before serving.

Chicken Wrap

Cal 392

Difficulty: Easy
Preparation time: 5 minutes
Cook time: 0 minutes
Servings: 4

Nutrition per serving (g)

Fat	Saturates	Carbs	Sugars	Fiber	Protein	Salt
12.7	4.7	17.7	3.5	5.5	22.7	0.2

Ingredients

- 1 ½ cups chicken, cooked and chopped
- 3 cups lettuce, chopped
- 20 cherry tomatoes, halved
- ¼ cup Parmesan, grated
- Pinch of pepper
- 4 gluten-free wraps, can substitute with other low-FODMAP-approved wraps

Method

1. In a bowl, mix together all the ingredients, leaving the wraps to the side.

2. Lay the wraps out and place ¼ of the mixture onto the center. Roll up. If taking to eat on the go, use a toothpick to secure the wrap.

Parmesan Mayo Corn on the Cob

Cal 254
VEGETARIAN

Difficulty: Easy
Preparation time: 5 minutes
Cook time: 10 minutes
Servings: 6

Nutrition per serving (g)

Fat	Saturates	Carbs	Sugars	Fiber	Protein	Salt
15	5.8	20	3.8	1.8	12.8	0.2

Ingredients

- 6 ears of corn, leaves still attached
- ½ cup mayonnaise
- ⅔ cup grated Parmesan
- 1 tbsp coriander, chopped

Method

1 In a pot of salted, boiling water, cook the corn for 7 minutes before draining. Leave to cool. Once cooled, pull back the leaves and place the corn onto a hot, greased skillet and grill for 5 minutes making sure to roll them until there are char marks.

2 In a bowl, mix the mayonnaise, Parmesan, and coriander. When the corn is ready, spread a tablespoon of the mayonnaise mixture onto each cob.

Serve warm.

Corn Salad

Cal 189 VEGAN	**Difficulty:** Easy **Preparation time:** 2 minutes **Cook time:** 5 minutes **Servings:** 2

Nutrition per serving (g)

Fat	Saturates	Carbs	Sugars	Fiber	Protein	Salt
8	1.5	17	10.5	5	5	0.5

Ingredients

- 1 can (15 oz) corn
- 1 cup cherry tomatoes
- 1 cup cucumber
- 2 spring onions, green parts only
- 1 red capsicum
- 2 tbsp mayonnaise (vegan)

Method

1 Slice the tomatoes in half.

2 Cut the cucumber into slices and then quarters. Chop the green part of the spring onion finely.

3 Thinly slice the capsicum.

4 Mix all the ingredients with the mayonnaise in a bowl and serve.

Hawaiian Toasted Sandwich

Cal 454

Difficulty: Easy
Preparation time: 4 minutes
Cook time: 6 minutes
Servings: 1

Nutrition per serving (g)

Fat	Saturates	Carbs	Sugars	Fiber	Protein	Salt
26.5	9.9	33.7	3	1.8	19.9	1

Ingredients

- 2 slices bread
- 1 tbsp butter
- 2 ½ tbsp pineapple chunks, drained
- 2 slices cheddar cheese
- 2 slices ham, cold cut
- 1 tbsp spring onion, tips finely chopped
- Pinch of black pepper

Method

1 Place a frying pan over medium heat.

2 Spread butter on the outside of each slice of bread.

3 Prepare the filling by grating the cheese, slicing the ham, rinsing the pineapple, and chopping the spring onion finely.

4 Put the sandwich together adding pepper to taste and ensuring the butter is on the outside.

5 Place in the frying pan and cook each side for 3 minutes. The bread should turn golden brown.

Serve warm

Frittata

Cal **519** VEGETARIAN	**Difficulty:** Easy **Preparation time:** 30 minutes **Cook time:** 25 minutes **Servings:** 4

Nutrition per serving (g)

Fat	Saturates	Carbs	Sugars	Fiber	Protein	Salt
27	11.8	45	11	8.3	25	0.9

Ingredients

Roast vegetables

- 2 medium sweet potatoes, cubed
- 4 large carrots, cubed
- 1 tbsp olive oil

Frittata

- 6 large eggs
- ½ cup lactose-free milk, can be substituted with coconut or almond milk
- 1 tsp thyme, dried
- Pinch of salt
- Pinch of pepper
- ½ cup spring onions, green part, thinly sliced
- 1 bell pepper, finely diced
- 1 cup broccoli, cut into florets
- 1 cup green beans
- ¾ cup cheddar cheese, can substitute other approved cheeses

Tomato relish

- ½ tbsp garlic-infused oil
- 1 cup leeks, green leaves only, sliced finely
- 2 large tomatoes, diced
- 2 tbsp tomato paste
- 1 tbsp red wine vinegar
- 1 tbsp white sugar
- 1 tbsp brown sugar
- Pinch of paprika, smoked
- Pinch of salt
- Pinch of pepper

Method

1. Preheat the oven to 425°F. Line a roasting tray with parchment paper. Place the sweet potatoes and carrots on the tray. Toss with oil and season to taste. Roast for 20 minutes until tender.

2. In a small pan over medium heat, fry the leek leaves in garlic-infused oil for 2 minutes. Add the other relish ingredients and let the mixture simmer for 15 minutes. It should reduce and thicken.

3. To make the frittata, whisk the eggs and milk together until smooth. If using feta crumble, put it into the egg along with the herbs.

4. Fry the spring onion and pepper in an ovenproof pan over medium heat for 2 minutes. Remove from the heat and mix with the vegetables. Pour the egg over the vegetables and top with cheese.

5. Bake in the oven for 20 minutes. It should have a golden appearance. Allow to stand for 5 minutes and serve with the relish.

Pesto Toasted Sandwich

Cal 555	**Difficulty:** Easy **Preparation time:** 5 minutes **Cook time:** 5 minutes **Servings:** 1

Nutrition per serving (g)

Fat	Saturates	Carbs	Sugars	Fiber	Protein	Salt
35	15	28	3	3	33	0.2

Ingredients

- 2 slices gluten-free bread
- 1 tbsp butter
- 1 tbsp pesto, no garlic or onion in the mixture
- 4 cherry tomatoes, halved
- 1 slice mozzarella
- ½ cup chicken breast, cooked and cubed

Method

1 Place a frying pan over medium heat.

2 Butter the outside of each slice of bread.

3 Mix together the filling ingredients and place onto the bread. Ensure the butter is on the outside of the sandwich when assembling.

4 Place the sandwich in the pan and fry for 3 minutes on each side. The bread should be golden.

Pineapple, Yogurt on Rice Cakes

Cal 169
VEGETARIAN

Difficulty: Easy
Preparation time: 5 minutes
Cook time: 12 minutes
Servings: 1 (2 rice cakes)

Nutrition per serving (g)

Fat	Saturates	Carbs	Sugars	Fiber	Protein	Salt
1.5	0.4	35.6	10	1.5	3.8	0

Ingredients

- 2 rice cakes
- ⅓ cup fresh pineapple, sliced
- 2 tbsp Greek yogurt
- ¼ tsp chia seeds, optional
- 1 tsp oil, used to prevent the pineapple from burning

Method

1 Spray the pineapple slices with oil, then place them on a tray in the oven and bake for 5 minutes on each side. Cut into chunky pieces.

2 Spread the yogurt over the rice cake and top with pineapple and chia seeds.

Quiche in Ham Cups

Cal 190

Difficulty: Easy
Preparation time: 10 minutes
Cook time: 20 minutes
Servings: 6

Nutrition per serving (g)

Fat	Saturates	Carbs	Sugars	Fiber	Protein	Salt
8.5	5.1	11.8	1.6	1.6	9.5	0.3

Ingredients

- 6 slices ham, cold cut, rounded
- 1 small bell pepper, diced
- ½ cup spring onion, green tips only
- 4 eggs, beaten
- 2 tbsp rice flour
- 4 tbsp lactose-free milk, can be substituted with other approved milk
- Pinch of salt
- Pinch of pepper

Method

1. Preheat the oven to 350°F and line 6 muffin tins with the ham slices.

2. Mix together the flour and milk, whisking constantly.

3. Add in the eggs, salt, and pepper, mixing until smooth. Add the spring onion and bell pepper. Pour carefully into the ham cups.

4. Bake for 15-20 minutes. It's ready when the quiche is puffy and the ham is crispy.

5. Let cool for 10 minutes then use a knife to carefully lift the quiche out of the tins.

Spring Rolls with Satay Sauce

Cal 472

VEGAN

Difficulty: Medium
Preparation time: 20 minutes
Cook time: 30 minutes
Servings: 3 (4 rolls per serving)

Nutrition per serving (g)

Fat	Saturates	Carbs	Sugars	Fiber	Protein	Salt
23.5	4.7	48.2	17	3.7	24.4	0.9

Ingredients

Satay sauce

- 4 tbsp peanut butter
- 2 tbsp lemon juice
- 2 tbsp water
- 2 tsp brown sugar
- 1 tsp white sugar

Rice spring rolls

- 12 rice paper wrappers
- 1 cucumber, small
- 1 carrot, large, cut into matchstick pieces
- 1 cup red cabbage, sliced finely
- ½ cup mint, fresh, chopped roughly
- ½ cup cilantro, fresh, roughly cut

Method

1 Prepare the satay sauce first. Soften the peanut butter in a microwaveable bowl for about 30 seconds. Place the rest of the sauce ingredients into the bowl and use a fork to mix until smooth. Add a tbsp of water if the mixture is too thick.

2 Put warm water into a large bowl. One at a time, dip a rice wrapper into the water until it softens slightly then place it on a clean, damp cloth.

3 Place a small amount of the fresh vegetables and herbs onto the bottom third of the wrapper. Do not overfill as it will affect the rolling process.

Thai Pumpkin Noodle Soup

Cal 373
VEGAN

Difficulty: Easy
Preparation time: 10 minutes
Cook time: 55 minutes
Servings: 6

Nutrition per serving (g)

Fat	Saturates	Carbs	Sugars	Fiber	Protein	Salt
16.3	12.3	52.6	8.1	7.7	7.4	0.6

Ingredients

Roast vegetables

- 3 ¼ cups pumpkin, peeled, deseeded, and cubed
- 1 cup carrots, peeled and cubed
- 1 tsp cumin, ground
- 2 tsp olive oil
- Pinch of salt
- Pinch of pepper

Soup

- 2 cups vegetable stock, without garlic or onion
- 1 cup spring onions, green part only, chopped finely
- 1 tsp ginger, crushed
- ½ tsp lemon zest
- 2 tsp soy sauce
- Pinch of chili flakes, to taste
- 1 ½ cups coconut milk, canned
- 1 cup thin rice noodles
- ¼ cup cilantro

Method

1. Preheat the oven to 350°F. Place the peeled and cubed pumpkin and carrots onto a roasting tray. Use the oil to coat the vegetables and season with cumin, salt, and pepper. Bake for 20-30 minutes, turning halfway. Remove when the vegetables are soft and golden.

2. Set the vegetables aside to cool for 10 minutes, and then blend them together with the stock until smooth.

3. Over medium heat, heat a saucepan, add some oil, and fry the spring onion for 3 minutes. Add the ginger. Let cook for another minute before adding the pumpkin and coconut milk.

4. Stir in the lemon zest, soy sauce, and chili flakes. Allow the soup to simmer for 10 minutes on low heat. Add water if the soup seems too thick.

5. Cook the noodles according to the instructions on the packet while the soup cooks. When cooked, stir the noodles into the soup with cilantro and serve.

Tomato and Green Bean Salad

Cal 125
VEGETARIAN

Difficulty: Easy
Preparation time: 3 minutes
Cook time: 5 minutes
Servings: 6

Nutrition per serving (g)

Fat	Saturates	Carbs	Sugars	Fiber	Protein	Salt
8.8	2	10.8	4.5	1.8	2.5	0.5

Ingredients

- 1 cup green beans
- ½ cup mayonnaise
- ½ cup Greek yogurt
- 1 tbsp chopped basil
- 2 tbsp chopped parsley
- Pinch of salt
- Pinch of pepper
- 2 tbsp lactose-free or another FODMAP-approved milk
- 1 tbsp Dijon mustard
- 2 tomatoes
- 2 spring onions, green part only
- 1 ½ cups lettuce

Method

1 In a bowl, mix mayonnaise, yogurt, milk, mustard, basil, parsley, salt, and pepper.

2 Wash the green beans, lettuce, and spring onions, then drain the water and chop the green onions. Shred the lettuce into a separate bowl and mix in the green beans and spring onions.

3 Cut the tomatoes into quarters and mix into the bowl. Put the dressing into a serving jug and serve.

Tropical Smoothie

Cal 434 VEGAN	**Difficulty:** Easy **Preparation time:** 2 minutes **Cook time:** 3 minutes **Servings:** 1

Nutrition per serving (g)

Fat	Saturates	Carbs	Sugars	Fiber	Protein	Salt
28	22	44	20	7	7	0.2

Ingredients

- ¾ cup frozen pineapple
- 1 cup baby spinach
- ½ tbsp lime juice
- ¾ cup ginger, ground
- ½ cup oat milk
- ½ cup coconut milk
- 1 tbsp flaxseed
- Pinch of salt

Mix the ingredients in a blender. Once the mixture has a smooth consistency, enjoy!

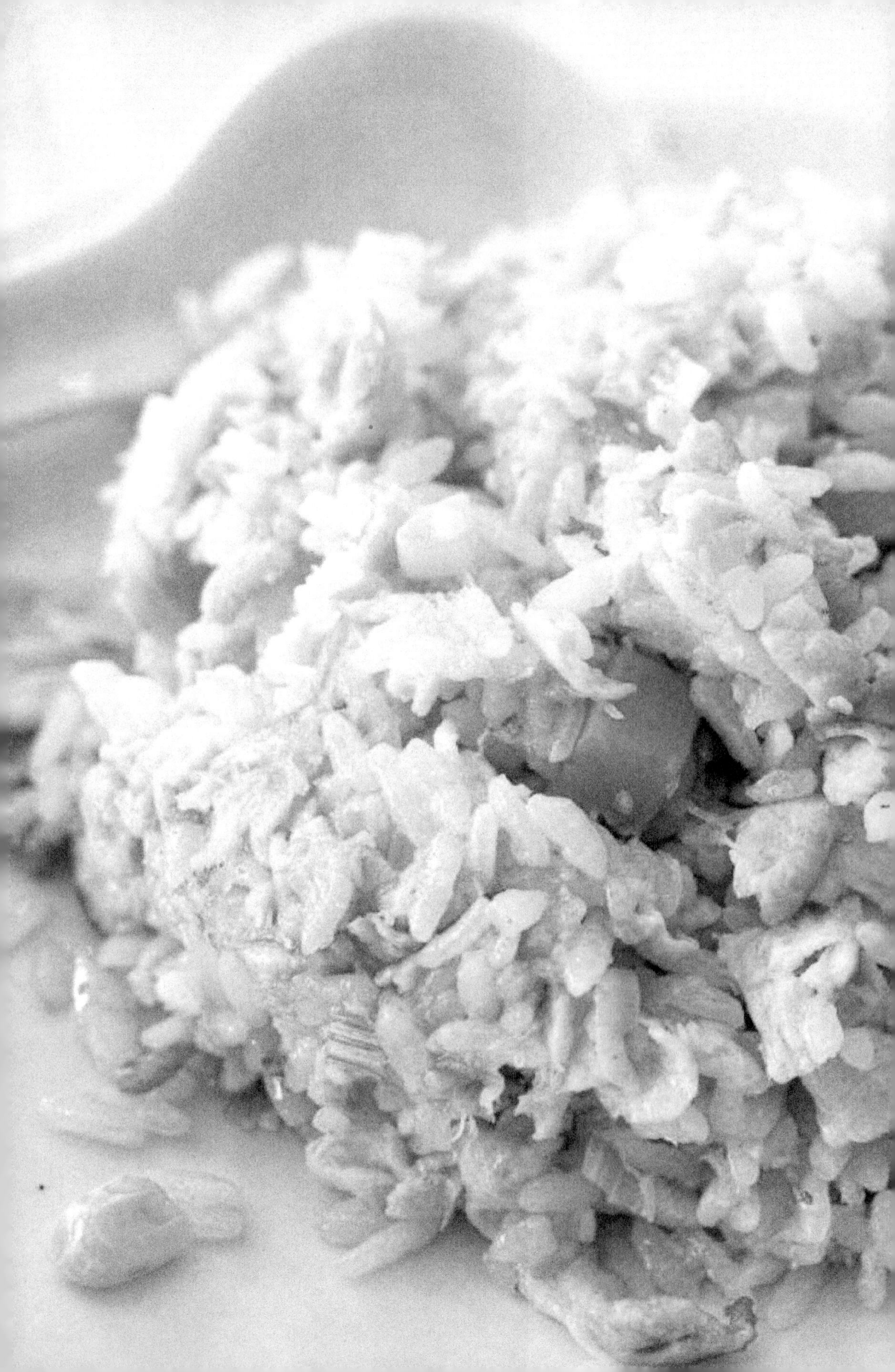

DINNER

Baked Chicken Alfredo ... 168

Bolognese ... 170

Burgers ... 172

Cheesy chicken ... 174

Coconut crusted fish ... 176

Day-Before Lamb Stew ... 182

Beetroot dip ... 178

Pesto noodles ... 184

Pork Tacos with Pineapple Salsa ... 186

Tofu Skewers ... 188

Tuna, bacon quinoa bowl ... 190

Vegetable Fried Rice ... 180

Zucchini fritters ... 192

Baked Chicken Alfredo

Cal 743

Difficulty: Easy
Preparation time: 35 minutes
Cook time: 15 minutes
Servings: 4 large servings

Nutrition per serving (g)

Fat	Saturates	Carbs	Sugars	Fiber	Protein	Salt
29	9	78.8	11	10	41	0.6

Ingredients

Pasta and chicken

- ½ lb chicken breast fillets, cut into chunks
- 1 tsp olive oil
- Pinch of salt
- Pinch of pepper
- 1 cup gluten-free pasta
- 4 cups baby spinach, chopped roughly
- 2 cups broccoli, florets
- ½ cup spring onion, green part
- ½ cup cheddar cheese
- 2 tbsp sage, fresh, chopped

Sauce

- 4 tbsp butter
- ¼ cup gluten-free flour
- 3 cups lactose-free milk
- ½ cup cheddar cheese
- 2 tbsp Parmesan, grated (optional)
- ½ tsp basil, dried
- Pinch of salt
- Pinch of pepper

Method

1 Preheat the oven to 350°F. Grease a large oven dish. Place a pot of water over medium heat to boil for the pasta.

2 Prepare the chicken by rubbing salt and pepper on it and then cutting into chunks. Chop the spinach, cut the broccoli, slice the spring onion, and grate the cheese.

3 Over medium heat, sear the chicken in a pan with oil and place to the side. Place the spinach in the pan and cook until slightly wilted, about 1 minute. Set to the side.

4 While the chicken cooks, place a saucepan over medium heat and melt the butter. Whisk in the flour. Cook for 1 minute, stirring continuously.

5 Whisk in ½ cup of milk. When smooth, whisk in the remainder of the milk a cup at a time. Season with salt, pepper, basil, and half the Parmesan. Stir occasionally and allow the sauce to thicken.

6 Cook the pasta for 5 minutes, then drain and toss with olive oil. Mix the pasta with the chicken, sauce, and vegetables. Transfer it into the oven dish, top with cheese, and bake for 10 minutes uncovered. Remove the lid of the dish and grill for 3 minutes and top with sage.

Bolognese

Cal 642

Difficulty: Easy
Preparation time: 5 minutes
Cook time: 40 minutes
Servings: 4

Nutrition per serving (g)

Fat	Saturates	Carbs	Sugars	Fiber	Protein	Salt
19	7.3	39.7	11	14.7	39.7	0.5

Ingredients

- 1 tbsp olive oil
- 1 lb ground beef, lean
- ½ cup leeks, tips only
- 1 can (14 oz) tomatoes, crushed
- 3 tbsp tomato paste
- 1 tsp oregano, dried
- 1 tsp thyme, dried
- 4 cups baby spinach
- Pinch of salt
- Pinch of pepper
- 1 ½ cups gluten-free spaghetti
- ½ cup approved cheese, grated
- 2 large carrots, peeled and cut into sticks
- ⅔ cup green beans

Method

1. Chop the spinach and leeks. Peel the carrots and cut into sticks. Slice the green beans. Put to one side.

2. Place a large pan over medium heat with olive oil in it. Cook the ground beef until it is browned. Add the tomatoes, leeks, spinach, and herbs to the beef. Mix well and let simmer for 20 minutes. Stir occasionally to ensure it does not burn. Season to taste.

3. In a large pot, add water and a generous amount of salt. Bring to a boil and add the spaghetti. Cook according to the packet instructions. Once cooked, drain and toss with olive oil.

4. Cook the green beans and carrots in a medium pot filled with boiling water for 2-3 minutes.

5. Serve the Bolognese on top of the spaghetti. Sprinkle with cheese and add the vegetables on the side.

Burgers

Cal 613	**Difficulty:** Easy **Preparation time:** 15 minutes **Cook time:** 30 minutes **Servings:** 4

Nutrition per serving (g)

Fat	Saturates	Carbs	Sugars	Fiber	Protein	Salt
22	5.6	62	19.6	12.7	39.9	0.9

Ingredients

Patties

- ½ lb ground beef, lean
- ¼ cup spring onion, green part, chopped finely
- ¼ cup gluten-free breadcrumbs (can be crumbled bread slices)
- 1 egg
- ½ tsp thyme, dried
- 1 tsp oregano, dried
- 1 tsp basil, dried
- 1 tbsp Worcestershire sauce
- Pinch of salt

Side salad

- 3 large carrots, peeled and cut into chunks
- 1 ½ tsp sunflower oil
- Pinch of salt
- Pinch of pepper
- 4 cups lettuce
- 1 cucumber, small
- 3 tomatoes, medium

Garnish

- 4 tbsp approved sauce, from the approved list
- 4 gluten-free buns

Method

1 Preheat the oven to 400°F. Place the peeled and cut carrots on a roasting tray with oil. Bake for 25-30 minutes, turning halfway through

2 To make the patties, first, whisk the egg in a small bowl. In a large bowl, mix the ground beef, spring onion, breadcrumbs, herbs, Worcestershire sauce, egg, salt, and pepper. Divide the mixture evenly into patties.

3 Fry the patties over medium heat for 7 minutes on each side.

4 Prepare the salad by washing and shredding the lettuce and chopping the tomatoes and cucumber.

5 Assemble the burger by placing the patties onto rolls. On the side, place the carrots and salad. Add an approved sauce onto the burger if desired.

Cheesy Chicken

Cal 661	Difficulty: Easy Preparation time: 15 minutes Cook time: 20 minutes Servings: 4

Nutrition per serving (g)

Fat	Saturates	Carbs	Sugars	Fiber	Protein	Salt
35	11	14	14	2.5	71	0.3

Ingredients

- 4 chicken breasts, deboned and skinned
- 2 tsp olive oil
- 1 tbsp garlic-infused oil
- 1 celery stalk, no more than 2 inches, chopped finely
- 1 carrot, chopped finely
- 1 can (15 oz) tomatoes, chopped
- 3 tbsp tomato purée
- 1 ½ tsp oregano, dried
- ⅓ cup olives, pitted
- 6 slices mozzarella cheese

Method

1 Season the chicken with salt and pepper and set aside. Grease a deep-frying pan with oil and put over high heat. Cook the chicken in the pan for 3 minutes on each side. When each side is brown, transfer them to a plate.

2 Reduce the heat to low and add more oil. Add the vegetables and cook for 5 minutes. Stir while cooking. When the vegetables are soft, cook with garlic-infused oil for a few seconds.

3 Add the tomatoes, tinned and puréed, and stir in the oregano and olives. Bring to a boil for 5 minutes, stirring regularly. Reduce the heat.

4 Preheat the grill to its maximum.

5 Let the sauce simmer gently and add the chicken. Cook for 10 minutes and season to taste.

6 Put the mozzarella slices on top of the chicken and sauce, and sprinkle on black pepper. Place on the grill for 3 minutes, letting the cheese melt.

Coconut Crusted Fish

Cal 480

Difficulty: Medium
Preparation time: 15 minutes
Cook time: 30 minutes
Servings: 4

Nutrition per serving (g)

Fat	Saturates	Carbs	Sugars	Fiber	Protein	Salt
20	7.4	42.7	8.1	7.7	33	0.2

Ingredients

Coconut crust
- ¼ cup dried coconut, shredded
- 2 tbsp sesame oil
- ¼ cup spring onion, finely sliced, green part only
- 1 mild chili, green
- 4 lime leaves
- 1 lb white fish (haddock/cod/coley)
- ½ cup cheddar cheese, can substitute other approved cheeses

Chips
- 5 potatoes, approximately 1 ½ lbs, sliced
- Pinch of salt
- Pinch of pepper
- 1 tbsp sunflower oil

Salad
- 1 small cucumber, peeled
- 4 cups lettuce, shredded
- ½ red bell pepper, deseeded and sliced
- 4 medium tomatoes, cut into wedges
- 1 lemon

Method

1 In a bowl, place the shredded coconut and cover with water. Leave to soak for 10 minutes and then drain the water.

2 Prepare the vegetables.

3 Pour half the sesame oil in a pan over medium heat. Fry the chili, spring onion, and lime leaves until they look caramelized. Add the coconut and fry for a minute more. Set aside in a bowl.

4 Put the remainder of the oil and half the potatoes into the pan. Fry until golden and cooked. Repeat with the rest of the potatoes. Season to taste.

5 To prepare the salad, wash, chop, and mix the ingredients together. Squeeze the lemon juice over top.

6 Turn the oven onto the grill function to heat up.

7 Grease a medium pan with oil and cook the fish for 2 minutes on each side. Move the fish to a baking tray and top with cheese and coconut crust. Grill for 2 minutes. The crust should be golden when ready.

Beetroot Dip

Cal 63
VEGAN

Difficulty: Easy
Preparation time: 5 minutes
Cook time: -
Servings: 6

Nutrition per serving (g)

Fat	Saturates	Carbs	Sugars	Fiber	Protein	Salt
4.6	4	5	3	1.6	1.1	0.1

Ingredients

- 1 ¼ cups baby beetroot, canned, drained
- 1 tbsp lemon juice
- 1 cup mint leaves, unchopped
- 1 tsp cumin seeds, whole
- ½ tsp fennel seeds
- ½ tsp coriander, ground
- ½ cup coconut yogurt, or other approved yogurts

Method

1. In a blender or food processor, place the beetroot, lemon juice, coriander, cumin, and fennel. Add the yogurt to the mixture and mix until the dip is smooth and at the desired consistency. The dip will thicken when it is cooled in the fridge.

2. Serve with plain chips, fresh vegetables, or rice crackers.

Vegetable Fried Rice

Cal **310** VEGETARIAN	**Difficulty:** Easy **Preparation time:** 5 minutes **Cook time:** 15 minutes **Servings:** 2

Nutrition per serving (g)

Fat	Saturates	Carbs	Sugars	Fiber	Protein	Salt
17.1	5.8	28.2	4.3	2.1	10.7	0.5

Ingredients

- 1 ½ cups rice, cooked and cooled
- 1 ½ tsp garlic-infused oil
- 2 eggs, whisked
- 2 carrots, chopped finely
- 2 cups vegetables (zucchini, bell peppers, and leeks), chopped into cubes
- 4 spring onions, green parts
- Pinch of salt
- 1 tbsp ginger, minced
- 2 tbsp sesame oil
- 1 tbsp soy sauce
- 1 tsp chili flakes, crushed

Method

1. In a large pan over medium heat, heat 1 tablespoon of garlic-infused oil. Add the egg, and cook until scrambled, stirring occasionally. Transfer the egg to another plate.

2. Heat the remaining ½ teaspoon of oil over medium heat, then add the carrots and other vegetables. Cook for 8 minutes until the carrot is soft.

3. Add the rice, onion, ginger, salt, and soy sauce to the pan. Stir for 3 minutes, then mix the egg into the dish.

4. Remove from the heat and stir in the sesame oil and chili flakes before serving.

Day-Before Lamb Stew

Cal 703

Difficulty: Difficult
Preparation time: 20 minutes
Cook time: 10 hours
Servings: 4

Nutrition per serving (g)

Fat	Saturates	Carbs	Sugars	Fiber	Protein	Salt
35.8	12.8	64	12	9	33.4	1.5

Ingredients

- ½ lb lamb, deboned
- 1 tbsp sunflower oil
- 1 ½ cups leeks, green tips
- 2 carrots, large
- 1 ½ cups pumpkin or sweet potato, cubed
- 3 cups potatoes, cubed
- 4 cups vegetable stock, no garlic or onion
- 1 cup boiling water
- 1 tsp oregano, dried
- ½ tsp thyme, dried
- Pinch of salt
- Pinch of pepper
- 1 cup green beans
- 3 tbsp parsley, fresh for garnish
- 8 slices gluten-free bread

Method

1 Use a slow cooker with cooking oil on low. Remove the fat from the lamb and cut into cubes.

2 In a frying pan over medium heat, brown the lamb for 5 minutes. Add the lamb to the slow cooker.

3 Clean the vegetables, peeling the sweet potato, carrots, and potato, then cutting them into cubes. Add to the slow cooker.

4 Add the garlic-infused oil, herbs, and heated vegetable stock into the slow cooker. Next, add the boiling water and season with pepper.

5 Cook the stew on low for 10 hours. Check the meat after 10 hours, and if it is soft, break the meat up softly with a fork to help it thicken.

6 Trim the green beans and place them into boiling water for 3 minutes before stirring into the stew. It is ready to be served.

7 Toast the bread and serve with a bowl of stew.

Pesto Noodles

Cal 569
VEGETARIAN

Difficulty: Easy
Preparation time: 5 minutes
Cook time: 10 minutes
Servings: 2

Nutrition per serving (g)

Fat	Saturates	Carbs	Sugars	Fiber	Protein	Salt
50	5.5	26	1.5	3	6	0.2

Ingredients

Pesto

- ¾ cup basil, fresh
- 2 tbsp garlic-infused oil
- ¼ cup pine nuts
- 2 tbsp olive oil
- Pinch of salt
- Pinch of pepper
- ½ cup Parmesan, grated

Noodles

- 1 cup rice noodles

Method

1 In a food processor, mix basil, garlic oil, and pine nuts until coarsely chopped.

2 Add the olive oil, cheese, salt, and pepper to the processor and mix until the pesto is fully mixed and smooth.

3 Cook the noodles according to the instructions on the packet. Once cooked, toss the noodles in a bowl with 3 tablespoons pesto and mix until the noodles are covered.

Serve!

Pork Tacos with Pineapple Salsa

Cal 210

Difficulty: Easy
Preparation time: 10 minutes
Cook time: 15 minutes
Servings: 6 (1 taco per serving)

Nutrition per serving (g)

Fat	Saturates	Carbs	Sugars	Fiber	Protein	Salt
5.8	1.5	19.6	7	2	20	0.2

Ingredients

Pork

- 1 tbsp garlic-infused oil
- 1 spring onion, green part
- 1 jalapeño, optional
- 2 tbsp soy sauce
- 1 lb pork loin, boneless, cut into thin strips
- 2 tbsp sugar
- 2 tbsp water

Pineapple salsa

- 1 cup pineapple, chopped
- 1 cup cucumber, chopped
- ½ cup cilantro, chopped
- ½ cup spring onion, green part, chopped
- 1 tbsp lime juice
- Pinch of salt
- 6 corn tortillas

Method

1. In a heavy pan, heat the garlic-infused oil over medium heat. Add the spring onion and jalapeño (optional) and cook for 2 minutes. Turn the heat up and add the soy sauce and pork to the pan. Fry for a few minutes until the pork has no pink.

2. Add the sugar and water. Stir. Wait a minute. Stir and repeat until the pork is golden brown.

3. Prepare the salsa by mixing the ingredients together in a bowl.

4. Warm the tortillas in a skillet with oil. Spread the pork and salsa between the tortillas.

Tofu Skewers

Cal 523

VEGAN

Difficulty: Easy
Preparation time: 10 minutes
(plus marinating overnight)
Cook time: 30 minutes
Servings: 4

Nutrition per serving (g)

Fat	Saturates	Carbs	Sugars	Fiber	Protein	Salt
15.9	2.2	70	9.8	5	25	1

Ingredients

Skewers

- 2 tbsp miso paste
- 1 tbsp garlic-infused oil
- 2 tbsp soy sauce
- ½ tsp crushed chili
- 1 ½ tbsp maple syrup
- 2 ½ cups (⅓ lb) tofu, firm, cubed
- 3 tsp sesame seeds for serving

Rice

- 1 ¼ cup basmati rice

Salad

- 3 cups lettuce
- 1 small cucumber, peeled and cut into chunks
- 1 cup spring onion, green tips, sliced finely
- 1 ⅓ cups green beans, cut in pieces
- 1 tbsp olive oil
- Juice from half an orange
- Pinch of salt
- Pinch of pepper

Method

1 Mix together the miso paste, garlic oil, soy sauce, chili, and maple syrup in a small bowl. Cover the tofu with half the marinade and soak overnight.

2 Preheat the oven to 375°F.

3 Cook the rice according to the instructions on the packet.

4 Prepare the salad by peeling and cutting the cucumber. Boil the green beans until bright green and then drain and rinse in cold water. Slice the spring onion tips. Toss the salad in a bowl with a drizzle of olive oil, orange juice, salt, and pepper.

5 On four skewers, divide the tofu. Bake in the oven for 12 minutes. When finished, the tofu should look caramelized.

6 Heat the remaining half of the marinade. Serve the skewers hot with sesame seeds used as a garnish and the rice and salad. Drizzle the remainder of the miso over the dish.

Tuna, Bacon Quinoa Bowl

Cal 288

Difficulty: Easy
Preparation time: 20 minutes
Cook time: 10 minutes
Servings: 2

Nutrition per serving (g)

Fat	Saturates	Carbs	Sugars	Fiber	Protein	Salt
6	1.5	34.5	1.5	3.5	22	0.3

Ingredients

Vinaigrette

- ½ cup olive oil
- 2 tbsp rice vinegar
- 2 tbsp lemon juice, fresh
- 1 tbsp Dijon mustard
- 1 tsp parsley, dried
- ½ tbsp garlic-infused oil
- Pinch of salt
- Pinch of pepper

Bowl

- 1 ½ cups quinoa, cooked
- ½ pack bacon
- 1 can (3 oz) of tuna, shredded, in brine
- 1 small cucumber, sliced
- ¼ cup cherry tomatoes, halved

Method

1 Combine the vinaigrette ingredients into a jar with an airtight lid. Shake well and let sit for 30 minutes before use.

2 Cook the quinoa according to the package instructions. Dice the bacon, and then fry it. Store all ingredients in separate containers.

3 Assemble each bowl by combining the ingredients and drizzling dressing over just before eating.

Zucchini Fritters

Cal **310** VEGETARIAN	**Difficulty:** Easy **Preparation time:** 10 minutes **Cook time:** 15 minutes **Servings:** 3 (2-3 fritters per serving)

Nutrition per serving (g)

Fat	Saturates	Carbs	Sugars	Fiber	Protein	Salt
17.2	5.8	28.2	4.3	2.1	10.7	0.5

Ingredients

Fritters

- 2 cups broccoli, cut into florets
- ¼ cup zucchini, grated
- ½ cup cheddar cheese, grated (other approved cheeses can be substituted)
- Pinch of salt
- Pinch of pepper
- 1 egg
- ½ cup gluten-free flour
- 3 tbsp lactose-free milk, can be substituted with other approved milk
- 1 tbsp garlic-infused oil

Lime aioli

- ¼ cup mayonnaise
- 2 tsp lime juice, fresh
- ½ tsp lime zest

Method

1. Cut the broccoli, steam it, then mash it. Grate the zucchini.

2. In a bowl, mix the wet ingredients. Add the dry ingredients, excluding the black pepper, into the bowl, then fold in the broccoli, zucchini, and cheese. Do not over mix.

3. Over medium heat, place a large pan that has been greased lightly with oil. With a ¼-cup measuring spoon, scoop some mixture and pour it into the pan then flatten gently with a spatula. Cook 2-3 fritters per batch.

4. Whisk the lime juice, zest, and mayonnaise and season with black pepper.

5. Serve the fritters topped with the aioli.

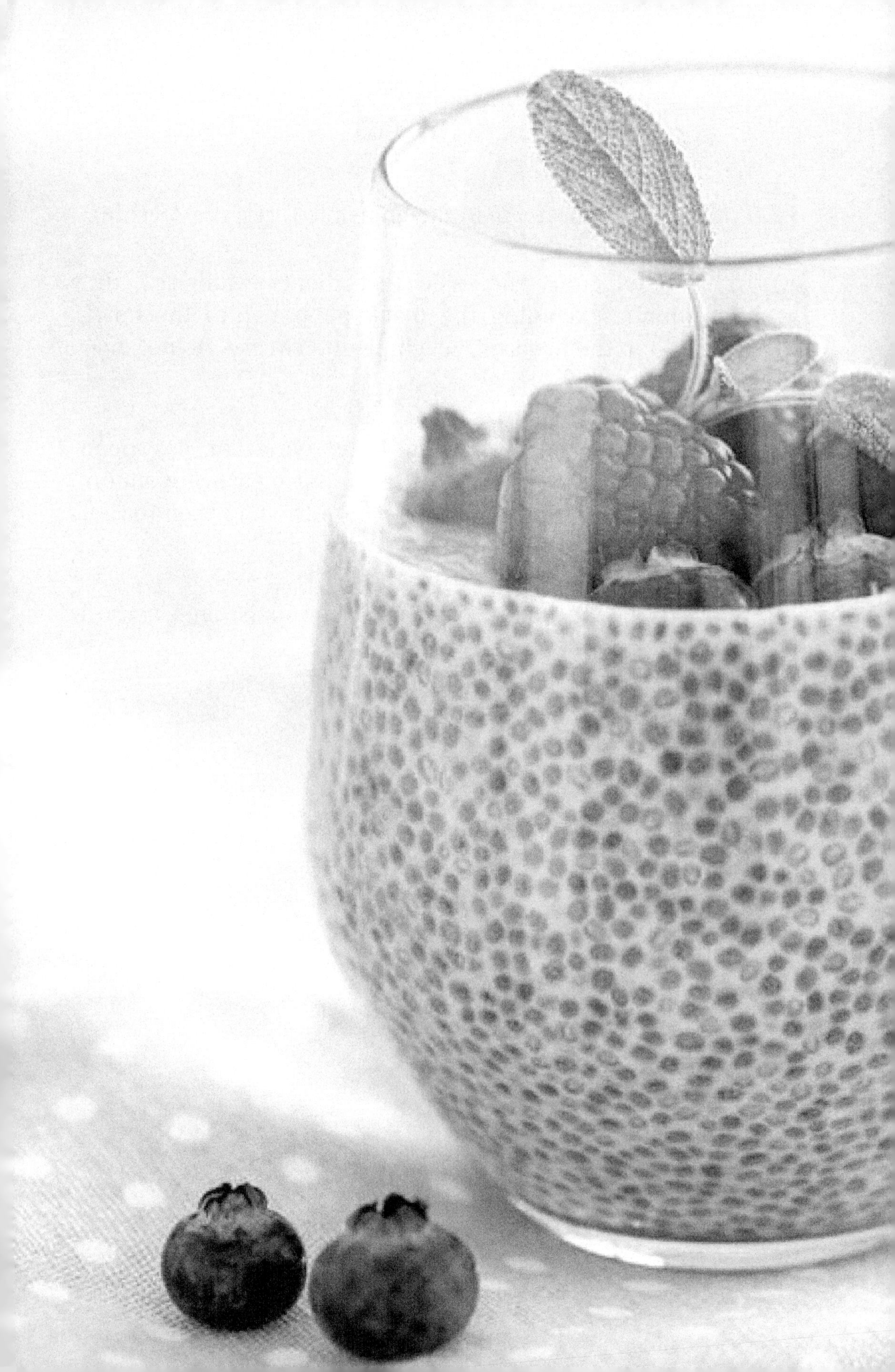

SNAKS

Chia pudding 196

Salted caramel pumpkin seed 198

Strawberry ice cream 200

Summer popsicles 202

Carrot Parsnip Chips 204

Chia Pudding

Cal 386

VEGAN

Difficulty: Easy
Preparation time: 8 minutes
Cook time: -
Servings: 3-4 (between ¼ and ⅓ of a cup per serving)

Nutrition per serving (g)

Fat	Saturates	Carbs	Sugars	Fiber	Protein	Salt
10	1	73	24	20	6	0.3

Ingredients

- ¼ cup chia seeds
- 1 tbsp cocoa powder
- 1 tbsp peanut butter
- 1 tbsp maple syrup
- 1 can coconut milk

Method

1 Fill an airtight jar with all the ingredients.

2 Close the jar and shake, then remove the top and stir the ingredients. Ensure that the bottom of the jar is clear. Shake again and place in the fridge for a minimum of 4 hours.

Salted Caramel Pumpkin Seeds

Cal 124 VEGETARIAN	Difficulty: Easy Preparation time: 5 minutes Cook time: 25 minutes Servings: 16 (2 tbsp per serving)

Nutrition per serving (g)

Fat	Saturates	Carbs	Sugars	Fibre	Protein	Salt
9.8	1.7	5.7	4	1.1	5.4	0.1

Ingredients

Roasted seeds
- 2 cups pumpkin seeds
- 2 ½ tbsp sugar
- ¼ tsp cinnamon, ground
- ½ tsp ginger, ground
- Pinch of nutmeg
- 2 tsp water

Salted caramel sauce
- 1 ½ tbsp butter
- 1 tbsp white sugar
- 1 ½ tbsp brown sugar
- ½ tsp rock salt

Method

1 Preheat the oven to 300ºF.

2 Mix the pumpkin seeds, spices, and sugar with water. The seeds should be damp to allow the spices and sugar to stick.

3 Line a tray with parchment paper and grease it. Spread the seeds evenly over the tray, then bake in the oven for 25 minutes. The seeds should be golden and crunchy. Remember to mix the seeds up halfway through cooking.

4 When the seeds finish baking, place a saucepan over medium heat and melt the butter. Mix the sugar and salt into the butter, then cook for 2 minutes until the mixture is a deep golden color. Lower the heat. Mix the seeds into the caramel, transfer back to the tray, and let cool.

Strawberry Ice Cream

Cal: 177

VEGAN

Difficulty: Easy
Preparation time: 15 minutes
Cook time: -
Servings: 4

Nutrition per serving (g)

Fat	Saturates	Carbs	Sugars	Fiber	Protein	Salt
4	3.5	37	28.4	2.7	1.2	0.1

Ingredients

- 2 small bananas, firm and frozen
- 7 oz strawberries, frozen
- 5 tbsp coconut yogurt
- 2 tbsp maple syrup
- 1 tsp vanilla extract

Method

1 Chop the frozen fruit into small pieces, then place the ingredients into a food processor. Blend until smooth, making sure to scrape down the sides.

2 Taste the mixture and add maple syrup or vanilla extract as desired. Serve soft or freeze for a few hours before serving. Serve with chocolate fudge sauce.

Summer Popsicle

Cal 156
VEGAN

Difficulty: Easy
Preparation time: 15 minutes
Cook time: 2 minutes
Servings: 4 (5 ½ tbsp per popsicle)

Nutrition per serving (g)

Fat	Saturates	Carbs	Sugars	Fiber	Protein	Salt
0.5	0.1	38.9	19.2	9.7	2.7	0.1

Ingredients

- 4 carrots, large
- 3 oranges, large
- 1 lime, juiced
- 1 tsp orange zest
- 2 tbsp powdered sugar

Method

1 Grate the carrots.

2 In a clean cloth, wrap the carrots and squeeze the juice into a bowl.

3 Zest an orange. Juice the oranges and lime into the bowl of carrot juice and mix the zest in. Add the powdered sugar. If the mixture tastes too sour, add more powdered sugar, then pour into popsicle molds.

4 Place in the freezer overnight. If using wooden sticks, place them in after 2 hours in the freezer.

Carrot Parsnip Chips

Cal **386** VEGAN	**Difficulty:** Easy **Preparation time:** 5 minutes **Cook time:** 35 minutes **Servings:** 3

Nutrition per serving (g)

Fat	Saturates	Carbs	Sugars	Fiber	Protein	Salt
10	1	73	24	20	6	0.3

Ingredients

- 1 large parsnip, peeled and ends cut off
- 1 large carrot, peeled and ends cut off
- 2 tsp olive oil
- Pinch of salt
- 1 tsp thyme leaves

Method

1 Preheat the oven to 325°F.

2 Oil a baking tray lightly.

3 Peel the carrot and parsnip into long thin pieces and place onto the tray. Drizzle with oil and season.

4 Cook for 35 minutes, turning the vegetables 2 times during cooking.

Conclusion

Are you still considering whether the low-FODMAP diet is right for you?

If you've been diagnosed with IBS, your doctor has probably ruled out any other potential gastrointestinal conditions you may have. Only then should you start the low-FODMAP diet. When you are diagnosed with IBS, you may experience various unwanted symptoms, such as bloating, gas, nausea, constipation, and diarrhea, all of which indicate that you need to make a lifestyle change. Since what we put into our body directly impacts our gastrointestinal tract and the proper functioning of our digestion, it is of utmost importance to adjust our diets according to what our bodies need. If you are diagnosed with IBS and experiencing one or more of the above-mentioned symptoms, the low-FODMAP diet could possibly be one of the best things that have ever happened to you. When you've reached a point of hopelessness in your disease, finding a way to combat your symptoms and recovering your balance with food while your condition improves accordingly, you'll surely feel like you've been granted a second chance at health again.

During this period, it's important to appreciate everything your body can do to support you, along with what it's already done for you. Since we only get one body, it can be challenging to accept that you're diagnosed with a condition that will never be cured, and although you can't do anything to rid yourself of it, you can adjust your daily habits and find ways to manage all the stress you are presented with to ultimately enjoy a better, more fulfilling lifestyle while living with IBS.

Others books by Robert Dickens

The Low-FODMAP diet cookbook

101 Easy, healthy & fast recipes for yours low-FODMAP diet

+ 28 days helpful meal plans

Vagus nerve secrets

Find out the secrets benefits of vagus nerve stimulation through self help exercises against trauma, anxiety and depression for better life!

References

All About FODMAPs: Who Should Avoid Them and How? (n.d.). Healthline. Retrieved

March 12, 2020, from https://www.healthline.com/nutrition/fodmaps#section1

Australia, H (2019, February 13). Low FODMAP diets. Www.Healthdirect.Gov.Au.

https://www.healthdirect.gov.au/low-fodmap-diets

Breit, S., Kupferberg, A., Rogler, G., & Hasler, G (2018). Vagus Nerve as Modulator of

the Brain–Gut Axis in Psychiatric and Inflammatory Disorders. Frontiers in Psychiatry, 9. https://doi.org/10.3389/fpsyt.2018.00044

Celiac Disease and IBS: Differences and Similarities - Celiac Disease Center (n.d.).

EverydayHealth.Com. Retrieved March 19, 2020, from https://www.everydayhealth.com/celiac-disease/celiac-disease-and-ibs-differences-and-similarities.aspx

Coping with irritable bowel syndrome (n.d.). Www.Medicalnewstoday.Com. Retrieved

March 21, 2020, from https://www.medicalnewstoday.com/articles/319546#5.-Consider-psychological-interventions

Cozma-Petruț, A., Loghin, F., Miere, D., & Dumitrașcu, D. L (2017). Diet in irritable

bowel syndrome: What to recommend, not what to forbid to patients! World Journal of Gastroenterology, 23(21), 3771. https://doi.org/10.3748/wjg.v23.i21.3771

Five Low FODMAP Diet Pitfalls (and What You Can Do to Avoid Them) (n.d.). Aboutibs.Org. Retrieved March 14, 2020, from https://aboutibs.org/low-fodmap-diet/five-low-fodmap-diet-pitfalls-and-what-you-can-do-to-avoid-them

Gastroparesis - Symptoms and causes (2018). Mayo Clinic. https://www.mayoclinic.org/diseases-conditions/gastroparesis/symptoms-causes/syc-20355787

How to Follow the Low-FODMAP Diet (n.d.). Verywell Health. Retrieved March 24,

2020, from

https://www.verywellhealth.com/how-to-follow-the-low-fodmap-diet-1944680

How to Improve Your Quality of Life With IBS (n.d.). Verywell Health. Retrieved

March 21, 2020, from https://www.verywellhealth.com/six-steps-for-having-a-life-with-ibs-1945130

How to Stimulate Your Vagus Nerve for Better Mental Health (n.d.).

https://sass.uottawa.ca/sites/sass.uottawa.ca/files/how_to_stimulate_your_vagus_nerve_for_better_mental_health_1.pdf

IBS or Lactose Intolerance: How Can You Tell? (n.d.). WebMD. Retrieved March 19,

2020, from https://www.webmd.com/ibs/guide/ibs-or-lactose-intolerance

Jackson, K (2018, April 24). 10 Things To Do Before Starting The Low FODMAP Diet.

Freelance Dietitians Group.

https://freelancedietitians.org/dietitian-blog-posts/10-things-to-do-before-starting-the-low-fodmap-diet/

Leiva, C (n.d.). 10 important things to know before starting the low-FODMAP diet.

Insider. Retrieved March 24, 2020, from

https://www.insider.com/fodmap-diet-what-to-know-2019-3

Images: www.freepik.com

Low-FODMap Diet Guide: Complete Scientific Guide | Everyday Health (n.d.).

EverydayHealth.Com. Retrieved March 24, 2020, from

https://www.everydayhealth.com/diet-nutrition/low-fodmap-diet/

National Institute of Diabetes and Digestive and Kidney Diseases (2020, January 12).

Symptoms & Causes of Irritable Bowel Syndrome | NIDDK. National Institute of Diabetes and Digestive and Kidney Diseases.
https://www.niddk.nih.gov/health-information/digestive-diseases/irritable-bowel-syndrome/symptoms-causes

Rossi, M (2017, March 15). A Beginner's Guide to the Low-FODMAP Diet. Healthline;

Healthline Media. https://www.healthline.com/nutrition/low-fodmap-diet

5 Simple Steps to Cure IBS Without Drugs (2010, September 16). Dr. Mark Hyman.

https://drhyman.com/blog/2010/09/16/5-simple-steps-to-cure-ibs-without-drugs/

The Low FODMAP Diet Step by Step (2018, February 15). For A Digestive Peace of

Mind—Kate Scarlata RDN.

https://blog.katescarlata.com/2018/02/15/low-fodmap-diet-step-step/

The Top 5 Benefits of Switching to a Low-FODMAP Diet this Year; Free yourself from

IBS (2017, January 4). Rachel Pauls Food. https://www.rachelpaulsfood.com/top-5-benefits-switching-low-fodmap-diet-2017/

Tips for Coping With IBS Symptoms (n.d.). HealthyWomen. Retrieved March 21,

2020, from https://www.healthywomen.org/content/article/tips-coping-ibs-symptoms

Ultimate Step-By-Step Guide to the FODMAP Elimination Phase IBS Health Coaching

and FODMAP Diet Recipes | Calm Belly Kitchen (n.d.). IBS Health Coaching and FODMAP Diet Recipes | Calm Belly Kitchen. Retrieved March 25, 2020, from https://calmbellykitchen.com/blog/step-by-step-guide-to-the-fodmap-elimination-phase

Vagus Nerve Stimulation and it's Many Benefits (2018, July 4). Mindd. https://mindd.org/vagus-nerve-stimulation-many-benefits/

What's a Low FODMAP Diet — And Is It Right for You? (2019, January 13). Brit + Co. https://www.brit.co/low-fodmap-diet/

What's the difference between IBS and IBD? (n.d.). Cedars-Sinai. Retrieved March 19,

2020, from https://www.cedars-sinai.org/blog/is-it-ibs-or-ibd.html

Printed in Great Britain
by Amazon